:RELOGO

promopress

# :RELOGO

Re-designing the brand
Pour repenser la marque
Rediseño de la marca
Per ridisegnare il marchio

Translators of the preface:
French / Spanish / Italian translator: Satèl.lit bcn - Olivier Gilbert / Miguel Izquierdo / Arrigo Frisano-Paulon

Copyright © 2011 by Sandu Publishing Co., Limited
Copyright © 2011 English language edition by
Promopress for sale in Europe and America.

PROMOPRESS is a commercial brand of:
Promotora de Prensa Internacional S.A.
C/ Ausiàs March, 124
08013 Barcelona, Spain
Phone: +34 93 245 14 64
Fax:     +34 93 265 48 83
info@promopress.es
www.promopress.info

Sponsored by: Design 360° – Concept and Design Magazine
Chief Editor: Wang Shaoqiang
Executive Editor: Wu Qiaohui
Chief Designer: Wang Shaoqiang
Book Designer: Leo Cheung
www.sandu360.com

ISBN: 978-84-92810-28-4

All rights reserved. No part of this publication may be reproduced or transmitted in any form or by any means, electronic or mechanical, including photocopy or any storage and retrieval system, without permission in writing from the publishers.

Tous droits réservés. La reproduction ou la transmission intégrale ou partielle du présent ouvrage ainsi que son stockage sur un système informatique, par quelque procédé que ce soit, électronique ou mécanique, ou par photocopie, téléchargement, enregistrement ou autre, faite sans le consentement écrit du détenteur du droit d'auteur est illicite.

Todos los derechos reservados. Esta publicación no puede reproducirse ni transmitirse en todo ni en parte, de ninguna forma ni por ningún medio, electrónico o mecánico, incluyendo fotocopia, grabación o cualquier sistema de almacenamiento, sin el permiso previo escrito del editor.

Tutti i diritti riservati. Questa pubblicazione non può essere riprodotta o trasmessa in tutto o in parte, in qualsiasi forma e con qualsiasi mezzo, elettronico o meccanico, incluse fotocopie, registrazioni o qualsiasi altro sistema di storage, senza il permesso scritto dell'editore.

Printed in China

# :PREFACE

## From old to New – How Things Have to Change

Gion-Men Kruegel-Hanna
Executive Creative Director of Interbrand

Welcome to *Relogo*, a wonderful publication that celebrates the new as well as the old. Each of the stories in this book takes us on a journey through the revitalisation of either a company, service, product or brand that is dear to us, wherever we may be. All of the cases found on these pages have two things in common: they each have their own heritage and legacy, and they all have undergone some sort of change. These range from subtle yet important modifications to a visual identity to the complete rebirth of a logo.

**A look around us.** Before we dig deeper into what change means to a brand in terms of form, attitude, nature and empowerment, it is well worth noting that the world we live in is in a state of constant flux and motion. At the same time it is in our nature as human beings to feel comfortable with the familiar, with what we have come to know and to cherish. Yet more and more, due to globalization and the ever-increasing presence of technology in our lives, we have to adapt ourselves to a rapidly changing world.

In terms of the companies portrayed in this book, whether small family businesses or large multinational corporations, all have spent many years establishing their values through how their brands behave as well as in the ways they look and feel. The same goes for tone of voice: how these brands speak, inform and approach their audiences and customers about their services or products is of equal importance. Furthermore, many of these companies have established long-lasting legacies through customer relationships and product portfolio expansion. Ranging from the coffee shop around the corner all the way to the identity of an entire city, these organizations have also encouraged staff to look beyond their initial endeavours to discover wider and broader areas with even bigger audiences with which to do business.

In addition, some of these companies have invested heavily in their brand's image and design because they understand that brand identity is not a necessary evil (i.e. something you don't really want to invest in but have to because everyone else does).

In fact, it is common knowledge nowadays that having a differentiating identity is a must in order to stand out, be seen and heard, and to be able to do increased and better business with more customers. This creates more value for the business.

**The path of change.** Change may well be the scariest path you can choose, but for survival in today's fast-paced world, it is also essential. It is crucial for a sustainable future, and the wellbeing and continued growth of our favourite brands depend on this progress. It means that we drive cars rather than sit in horse carriages and that we fire off quick texts rather than pick up the phone. Change has also had a huge impact on how we travel around the world, how we access what we need for our daily happiness, and how we see, smell and hear new cultures that were previously unknown to us.

You can also argue that change and globalization have brought us many challenges, which are sometimes difficult to manage and even to comprehend. Yet by the same token, change today means that if someone drops a pin in the remotest corner of the earth, we can hear about it almost instantaneously wherever we may be. Whether good or bad, that's simply the way it is. So, let's focus on the good and seize the opportunities that lay at hand.

**Is playing it safe the answer?** The big question is: how much safer is it to carry on within our comfort zones? We all know that positive change can quickly drop from the agenda when managers have dozens of projects piling up on their desks. A blinkered, conveyor-belt mentality can take over quickly. When the stakes of winning a pitch or launching a new product are high, the temptation is to churn out whatever may have succeeded last time. When shareholder demands, the bottom line or even survival itself becomes top priority in a difficult economic environment, risk-takers are often shown the door. In the short term, this limited strategy might allow the company to muddle through. Employees will deliver the same old results in a robotic way, without inspiration or new rationales. But creativity soon stagnates. "We've always done it this way" and "We don't have enough time" become mantras.

**Change is empowerment.** In fact, doing things differently – in a more inspiring way and discovering unchartered territories – is what change is all about. We can find fruitful and exciting new stimuli along the way. When put into the right context, these can rapidly propel a business forward. Change is the single and most potent motivating factor for employees and brand owners. It is what separates stagnation from standing out.

This is the kind of change *Relogo* is all about. It celebrates how a first glimpse of an idea, a glimmer in someone's imagination, can spark a powerful flame. It is about true differentiation and the strong identities that make these brands stand out. It is also about embracing new technologies and giving the consumer a better understanding of what is going on around them and what makes the world go round. In these pages, you will find inspiring ways of achieving change and in-depth information about what it means to be fresh and vivid, as well as how to give a brand identity a new set of 'clothes'.

In closing, I hope that reading *Relogo* will take you on an exciting journey. Embrace the new and leave the old behind in order to embark on an adventure of revitalized brand identities, all of which have undergone small, medium or big – yet always significant – change.

So long – embrace the change.

# A Logo Does Not Make a Brand Identity

Joe Duffy
Chairman of Duffy & Partners

The first logo was designed sometime in the late 1800s. I myself have been creating brand identities for over 30 years, so it might seem strange to hear that I think most people in the design business put way too much stock in "logos." In fact, I think they're highly overrated. As much as I appreciate the distillation of a brand's essence into a simple graphic device, even when it's done properly (which is rare by the way) it is only one of many "moving parts" that successfully create a connection between a brand and its intended audiences.

What successful brands need is a complete "language"—one that is unique, ownable and relevant to the people they care about most. This language must be three-dimensional, at the very least. It should consider how a brand looks, sounds, feels and perhaps even smells and tastes. It must convey, in honest terms, why the brand exists and how it suits its participants. A brand language is an invitation for people to join a cause as much as it is about marketing, transactions or consumerism. And frankly, it is impossible to do all this with a logo.

Think of the logo as the pivot point of the brand's language. It is a signature of sorts, and should be one that relates to the characteristics of the "person" doing the signing. It may start with looks but it certainly shouldn't end there. If we continue with the analogy of a person, the characteristics of the logo and its more complete brand language will tell a story of a belief system. It should do so in a particular style—just as people might dress themselves and share their ideas— and in so doing, engage friends and others who are attracted to similar things.

If designers are to make a real business impact with brand design, they must think beyond than the logo. In my opinion, the creative process should neither begin nor end with the logo. It should really begin with observation. It is through curiosity that we see things differently. The creative process is as much about interrogating a brand's history and the culture of the people behind its products or services and understanding the competitive set and the brand's place in people's lives, as it is about the creation of graphic devices. Importantly it's about being aware of culture and how a brand lives in the world.

All too often I've seen a designer follow the initial inclination to dismantle an existing identity and begin a new logo design from scratch. I believe that's ego at play. The more respectful, more appropriate tactic is to study the past and existing: to analyse heritage and identify negative baggage, as well as positive equities, and build from there.

Over the years, some of our most successful brand identity work has been with brands where the pre-existing logo was left untouched or perhaps evolved, refreshed or revitalised. As designers we all want to make an impact. We aspire to leave a legacy. Our clients and business partners want the same. And so as we work to design logos and develop brand languages to create meaningful brand identities, we must consider the role of the logo as just one element. The logo is like a signature: important, personal and unique. Like its maker, the signature may evolve with time, but any changes should be reflective of its place in the context of the community and broader culture in which it exists.

I believe the best designers are truly students of culture, trends, and of their craft. As such, this book aims to offer a contribution to your studies of logos, how they are created and evolve, and their role in brand language and in creating brand identities, which will stand the test of time with meaning and impact.

# Logo Remake

Wu Qiaohui
Executive Editor

A logo is the visual representative of a brand. Nike, Apple and Chanel are all easily associated with a tick, a bitten apple and two symmetrical letter Cs interlaced together, respectively... When talking about a certain brand, the logo emerges in people's mind. This is the logo's visual identity function. As a matter of fact, logo and brand supplement each other. An excellent logo gives a brand a unique visual image; while conversely, a brand's success elevates its logo's connotation.

Time changes, evolving trends and fierce competition have brought about many brands' drive to redesign their logo in recent years. And new logos play a fundamental role in retargeting clients, promoting the brand and raising its prestige, for which reason a series of visual images of the brand must be designed, centring on the logo.

Redesigning a logo is a risky enterprise. Excellent and well-accepted logo design can benefit the brand. However, if the new logo is not accepted by the public, as a result of an ingrained impression of the old logo, not only will the new logo be criticised, but also the brand itself will find itself facing a dilemma. Compared with designing a brand new logo, redesigning a logo seems to be more difficult. For the sake of people's approval, the new logo needs to outstrip the success of the old one, breaking new ground and surprising people by offering a brand new visual experience.

There are three kinds of paths for developing different logo redesign projects. First is redesigning the logo on the basis of adapting some elements of the old logo, such as colour, figure, typeface, etc. Second off, there is the possibility of completely breaking the limitations of the old logo by applying a totally different one, presenting the brand in a whole new light. A third option involves creating a series of logos based around the same theme but with diverse visages. Changeability and flexibility can well express the brand's vigour and vitality and its different aspects.

The quality of the logo design itself is a very important criterion for judging the logo. But after years of development and evolution, today logo design is not restricted to the scope of the logo itself, but also encompasses further application design beyond the logo. Some logo designs are outstanding in themselves, successfully reflecting the characteristics of the brand, elaborating the brand's management philosophy and catching people's eyes, while some are not so impressive, but manage to achieve a similar effect in conjunction with additional application design.

Besides featuring abundant logo work, *Relogo* discusses the challenges faced by brands and the difficulties posed to designers by the inclusion of client briefs and the influence of design philosophies established by design agencies. Readers can understand the stories behind the brands, and obtain an extensive and valuable source of inspiration.

# :PRÉFACE

## De l'ancien ou nouveau – comment adopter le changement

Gion-Men Kruegel-Hanna
Directeur de création d'Interbrand

Bienvenu à *Relogo*, une publication extraordinaire qui célèbre le nouveau ainsi que l'ancien. Chacune des histoires racontées dans ce livre est un voyage à travers la revitalisation d'une compagnie, d'un service, d'un produit ou d'une marque qui nous sont chers, où que nous soyons. Tous les exemples révélés sur ces pages possèdent deux facteurs communs : ils ont chacun leur propre patrimoine et héritage, et ils ont tous subi un changement d'identité visuelle qu'il soit subtil mais significatif ou l'inverse global par un renouveau complet du logo.

**Un regard autour de nous.** Avant d'approfondir ce que signifie ces changements pour une marque en matière de forme, d'attitude, de nature ou de notoriété, il est important de prendre conscience que le monde dans lequel nous vivons est en mutation et mouvement constant. Dans le même temps, comme êtres humains, nous avons tendance à nous sentir satisfaits avec ce qui nous est familier, ce que nous avons appris à connaître et à apprécier. Or de plus en plus, en raison de la mondialisation et de la présence toujours croissante de la technologie dans nos vies, nous devons nous adapter rapidement à un monde en perpétuelle évolution.

Les entreprises décrites dans ce livre, qu'il s'agisse de petites entreprises familiales ou de grandes multinationales, ont passé de nombreuses années à consolider leurs valeurs à travers le comportent de leurs marques c'est à dire la façon dont elles se perçoivent et se ressentent. Il en va de même pour le ton de voix : Il est d'égale importance la manière avec laquelle ces marques s'expriment, informent et approchent leur public et leurs clients sur leurs produits ou leurs services. De même, beaucoup de ces entreprises ont forgé une empreinte durable à travers leurs relations clientèle et la croissance de leur portefeuille de produits. Du café du coin en passant par une ville entière, ces organisations ont également encouragé leur personnel à étendre leurs missions initiales afin d'élargir leur clientèle et de s'ouvrir sur des marchés plus amples et plus diversifiés.

De plus, certaines de ces entreprises ont investi lourdement dans leur image de marque et dans leur design, car elles comprennent que l'identité de marque n'est pas juste un mal nécessaire – soit quelque chose d'indispensable mais subi contraint et forcé pour suivre la concurrence.

De fait, il est de notoriété publique aujourd'hui que se démarquer par son identité est une nécessité afin d'être vu et entendu, et d'être capable de faire croître en qualité et quantité ses affaires par une clientèle élargie. Il s'agit réellement de créer davantage de valeur pour l'entreprise.

**La voie du changement.** Le changement est peut-être le chemin le plus inquiétant, mais pour survivre dans un monde effréné, il est indispensable. Cette évolution est cruciale pour un avenir durable et une croissance continue et prospère de nos marques préférées. Il en résulte que nous conduisons des voitures plutôt que des calèches et que nous envoyons des textos plutôt que de décrocher le téléphone. Le changement a aussi eu un impact énorme sur la façon dont nous voyageons à travers le monde, sur comment on accède à nos besoins pour notre bonheur quotidien, et sur comment nous voyons, sentons et écoutons de nouvelles cultures qui étaient auparavant inconnues de nous.

Vous pouvez également faire valoir que le changement et la mondialisation nous ont apporté de nombreux défis, qui sont parfois difficiles à gérer et même à comprendre. Pourtant et par la même occasion, le changement signifie aujourd'hui que si quelqu'un fait tomber une épingle à l'autre bout de la terre, cette information peut nous parvenir presque instantanément où que nous soyons. Que cela soit bénéfique ou néfaste, c'est simplement la réalité d'aujourd'hui. Alors, concentrons-nous sur le coté bénéfique et saisissons les opportunités qui se trouvent à portée de mains.

**Jouer sûr est-elle la réponse?** La grande question est : Jusqu'à quel point est-il plus sûr de perdurer au sein de nos sphères de confort? Nous savons tous que des changements positifs peuvent rapidement disparaître de l'ordre du jour étant donné les dizaines de projets s'accumulant sur les bureaux des gestionnaires, de telle sorte qu'une tendance à l'inertie et une mentalité court-termiste peuvent rapidement s'imposer. Lorsque les enjeux, liés à une prise de contrôle d'une autre société ou le lancement d'un nouveau produit, sont élevés, la tentation est grande de reproduire à la hâte les idées à succès du passé. Devant les exigences des actionnaires et dans un environnement économique difficile, la première priorité est la rentabilité ou la survie elle-même de l'entreprise et dans ce cas les preneurs de risques sont souvent mis à la porte. A court terme, cette stratégie limitée peut permettre à l'entreprise de s'en sortir. Les employés donneront les mêmes résultats avec constance et automatisme sans inspiration ni nouvelles perspectives. Mais la créativité rapidement s'en trouvera lésée. «Nous avons toujours fait comme ça» et «Nous n'avons pas assez de temps" deviendrons les mantras.

**Le changement par l'autonomie.** En fait, faire les choses différemment - de façon plus inspirée en découvrant des territoires inexplorés – c'est l'essence du changement. Sur ce chemin nous trouverons des stimulations nouvelles et bénéfiques, qui utilisées dans le bon contexte pourront rapidement propulser une entreprise vers l'avant. Le changement est le facteur de motivation le plus puissant pour les employés et les propriétaires de marques. C'est ce qui sépare la paralysie de l'excellence.

*Relogo* traite justement de ce type de changement. Il célèbre l'étincelle d'une idée qui scintille dans l'imagination de quelqu'un pour déclencher un brasier. Il traite des véritables différentiations et des identités fortes qui font que ces marques sont uniques. Il met l'accent sur les nouvelles technologies et donne au consommateur les clefs de ce qui se passe autour d'eux et de ce qui fait tourner le monde. Dans ces pages, vous trouverez les moyens pour insuffler le changement et une information détaillée sur ce que cela signifie d'être vivant et alerte, ainsi que la façon de donner à une identité de marque un nouvel esprit.

En définitive, j'espère que la lecture de *Relogo* évoquera un voyage passionnant vers l'adoption du nouveau et l'abandon de l'ancien. Nous embarquerons dans l'aventure des identités de marque revitalisées, qui ont toutes subi des petits, moyens ou grands- mais toujours significatifs - changements.

Bon voyage - sur les allées du changement.

# Il ne suffit pas d'un logo pour créer une identité de marque

Joe Duffy
Président de Duffy & Partners

Le premier logo a été conçu vers la fin du XIX siècle. Pendant plus de 30 ans, je me suis moi-même consacré à créer des identités de marque, il peut donc sembler étrange de m'entendre dire que la plupart des gens dans le monde du design attache trop d'importance aux logos. En fait, je considère qu'ils sont surévalués. Pour autant que j'apprécie la distillation de l'essence d'une marque grâce à un simple symbole graphique, je dois dire que même quand c'est fait correctement (ce qui est d'ailleurs rare), il est seulement un des nombreux «éléments mobiles» destinés à créer une connexion entre une marque et sa clientèle ciblée.

Ce dont les marques à succès ont besoin c'est d'un "langage" complet – unique, que l'on peut s'approprier et judicieux pour le public dont elles se soucient le plus. Ce langage doit être au minimum en 3 dimensions. Il doit envisager comment une marque se voit, s'entend et se touche et même comment elle se sent et se savoure. Il doit transmettre honnêtement pourquoi la marque existe et combien elle est bénéfique pour ceux qui y adhèrent. Un langage de marque est autant une invitation à rejoindre une cause qu'une question de marketing, de balance commerciale ou de consommation. Et sincèrement, un logo seul ne peut répondre à l'ensemble de ces problématiques.

Pensez le logo comme le pivot autour du quel tourne le langage de marque. C'est une sorte de signature qui devrait être reliée aux caractéristiques de la «personne» qui l'exécute. Son apparence peut être un début, mais cela ne peut certainement pas s'arrêter là. Si nous continuons l'analogie avec une personne, les caractéristiques du logo et son langage de marque doivent façonner un système de croyance et le faire dans un style particulier – tout comme les gens peuvent s'habiller et partager leurs idées – attirant toutes personnes qui possèdent une affinité pour des choses similaires.

Si les designers aspirent à obtenir un réel impact économique grâce au design d'une marque, ils doivent penser au-delà du seul logo. A mon avis, le processus créatif ne doit ni commencer ni se terminer par le logo. Il faut vraiment commencer par l'observation. C'est la curiosité qui nous pousse à voir les choses différemment. Le processus créatif se traduit autant par le questionnement sur l'histoire d'une marque et sur la culture d'entreprise des hommes et femmes derrières ses produits ou ses services, ou par la compréhension du milieu concurrentiel et de la place de la marque dans la vie des gens, que par la création de nouvelles ressources graphiques. Il est important de s'ouvrir sur les cultures et de savoir comment vit une marque dans un contexte mondialisé.

J'ai vu trop souvent des designers ayant tendance de prime abord à faire table rase de l'identité existante et à se lancer dans la création d'un nouveau logo à partir de zéro. L'égo, il me semble, n'a pas de place dans ce processus créatif. Il existe une approche plus respectueuse et plus appropriée : étudier l'existant pour analyser les points positifs et négatifs de l'héritage identitaire et définir à partir de là de nouvelles fondations.

Au fil des ans, une grande partie de nos projets couronnés de succès sur l'identité d'entreprise a été mené avec des sociétés dont le logo a été laissé intact, ou le cas échéant légèrement retouché, ravivé ou revitalisé. Nous autres les designers prétendons toujours provoquer un certain impact et voulons tous laisser une empreinte. Nos clients et partenaires commerciaux aspirent aussi à cela. Dans cette logique, lors de la création d'une identité de marque, à travers la conception du logo et le développement du langage de marque, nous devons considérer le rôle du logo comme un parmi d'autres. Le logo est la signature: importante, personnelle et unique. Comme son créateur, il doit évoluer au fil du temps, et tous les changements doivent renvoyer à la place qu'il occupe dans la communauté et la culture à lesquelles il appartient.

Je crois fermement que les meilleurs designers doivent se consacrer à l'examen attentif de la culture, des tendances et des arts rattachés. En ce sens, ce livre doit jouer un rôle dans vos études sur les logos : comment sont-ils créés et évoluent-ils ? Quel est leur rôle dans la définition d'un langage de marque et dans la création d'identités d'entreprise qui résistent à l'épreuve du temps avec force de persuasion et respect des valeurs ?

# Repenser le logo

Wu Qiaohui
Directeur Editorial

Un logo est la représentation visuelle d'une marque. Nike s'associe facilement à la virgule posée à l'envers et à l'horizontale, le « swoosh », Apple à une pomme croquée et Chanel au double C symétrique et entrelacé. Quand on parle d'une marque, le logo apparaît immédiatement à l'esprit des gens. C'est précisément la fonction d'identité visuelle du logo. De fait, le logo et la marque se complètent mutuellement. Un logo bien conçu procure à une marque une image visuelle univoque, et réciproquement, le succès d'une marque fortifie la perception de son logo.

Le progrès, l'évolution des tendances et la concurrence féroce ont poussé de nombreuses marques à repenser leur logo. Un nouveau logo joue un rôle fondamental afin de cibler une nouvelle clientèle, de promouvoir une marque et d'accroître son prestige. C'est pour ces raisons qu'une sélection de représentations visuelles de la marque doit être conçue à partir du logo.

Repenser un logo est une entreprise risquée. Une marque peut tirer profit d'un excellent logo qui soit bien accueilli par le marché. Toutefois, si le nouveau logo n'est pas adopté par le public, en raison de l'ancien logo enraciné dans l'esprit des gens, non seulement le nouveau logo sera critiqué, mais la marque elle-même se trouvera face à un dilemme. Les contraintes qu'implique la refonte d'un logo semblent bien plus complexes que celles rencontrées lors de la conception d'un nouveau logo. Pour obtenir l'approbation du public, le nouveau logo a besoin de surpasser la popularité de l'ancien, en cassant les idées reçues et en surprenant les gens afin de leur offrir une nouvelle expérience visuelle de la marque.

Il y a trois sortes de voies pour mener à bien le développement de projets destinés à réactualiser un logo. La première est la refonte du logo sur la base de l'adaptation de certains éléments de l'ancien, comme la couleur, la forme ou la police de caractère, etc. La deuxième passe par la possibilité de briser complètement le cadre de l'ancien logo et en créer un totalement différent pour ainsi donner à la marque de nouvelles perspectives. Une troisième option consiste à créer une série de logos basés autour du même thème mais avec différentes apparences. La variabilité et la flexibilité sont des facteurs qui peuvent exprimer ainsi la force et la vitalité de la marque et ses diverses facettes.

La qualité du design du logo en soi est un critère déterminant pour le juger. Mais après des années de développement et d'évolution, actuellement, le design du logo ne se limite pas au logo lui-même, mais englobe aussi celui d'autres applications qui le complètent. Certains designs de logo sont remarquables en eux-mêmes, reflétant avec succès les caractéristiques de la marque, exprimant la philosophie de gestion de la marque et captivant l'attention du public, alors que d'autres, moins percutants, parviennent finalement à obtenir un effet similaire grâce à ces autres applications.

En plus de présenter nombreuses réalisations de logo, *Relogo* examine les défis auxquels sont confrontés les marques et les difficultés posées aux designers par les désidératas des clients et l'influence des philosophies de design établies par les agences. Les lecteurs peuvent ainsi comprendre l'histoire derrière la marque et obtenir une source d'inspiration abondante et précieuse.

# :PRÓLOGO

## De lo viejo a lo nuevo: de qué modo deben cambiar las cosas

Gion-Men Kruegel-Hanna
Director ejecutivo creativo de Interbrand

Bienvenidos a *Relogo*, una publicación extraordinaria que rinde homenaje a lo nuevo tanto como a lo antiguo. Cada una de las historias de este libro es un viaje a través de la revitalización de una empresa, un servicio, un producto o una marca con los que, estemos donde estemos, sentimos cierta afinidad. Todos los casos registrados en estas páginas tienen dos cosas en común: cada cual cuenta con su propia herencia y legado y todos ellos han sufrido algún tipo de modificación, que tanto puede ser una alteración sutil aunque significativa de la identidad visual, como una plena refundación del logo.

**Una mirada en derredor.** Antes de profundizar en lo que un cambio significa para una marca en términos de forma, actitud, esencia y capacitación, cabe notar que el mundo en el que vivimos se halla en un estado de flujo y movimiento constantes. Al mismo tiempo, como seres humanos tendemos a sentirnos cómodos con lo que nos es familiar, aquello que hemos acabado por conocer y apreciar. Con todo, debido a la globalización y a la presencia cada vez mayor de la tecnología en nuestras vidas, debemos adaptarnos con mayor prontitud a un mundo siempre cambiante.

Las empresas retratadas en este libro, bien sean negocios familiares o grandes corporaciones multinacionales, han pasado largos años consolidando sus valores a través del comportamiento de sus marcas, así como de su apariencia y percepción. Lo mismo vale para el tono de voz: el modo en que estas marcas hablan, informan y enfocan a su público y clientes acerca de sus servicios o productos es de igual importancia. De otra parte, muchas de estas empresas cuentan con un legado duradero fundado a partir de la relación con los clientes y de la expansión de su catálogo. Desde la cafetería de la esquina a la identidad de una ciudad entera, tales entidades han alentado también a su personal a trascender sus tareas iniciales para hacer negocios en áreas más extensas con públicos más amplios.

Además, algunas de estas empresas han invertido cuantiosas sumas de dinero en su imagen y diseño de marca porque entienden que la identidad corporativa no es necesariamente un engorro, esto es, algo en lo que no se quiere invertir pero se hace porque es práctica común.

De hecho, hoy día todos sabemos que contar con una identidad diferenciada es un imperativo si se desea destacar, ser visto y escuchado, y poder aumentar y mejorar el negocio con un mayor número de clientes. Se trata de crear valor para la empresa.

**La senda del cambio.** El cambio es quizá el camino que más asusta, pero para sobrevivir en un mundo de ritmo endiablado, resulta crucial. Es capital para un futuro sostenible en que el bienestar y el crecimiento continuado de nuestras marcas favoritas dependen de dicho progreso. Eso es lo que implica conducir coches en lugar de trasladarnos en calesas e intercambiar mensajes de texto inmediatos en lugar de coger el teléfono. Los cambios tienen también un impacto colosal en el modo en que viajamos por el mundo, en cómo accedemos a lo que precisamos para nuestra felicidad cotidiana y en cómo vemos, olemos y oímos nuevas culturas que nos eran desconocidas.

Se puede argumentar que los cambios y la globalización han acarreado grandes desafíos, que a menudo resultan difíciles de gestionar e incluso de asimilar. De igual manera, sin embargo, el cambio significa que podamos oír casi instantáneamente, estemos donde estemos, un alfiler que cayó en la esquina más remota de la tierra. Para bien o para mal, así están las cosas. De modo que centrémonos en lo bueno y aprovechemos las oportunidades que se presentan.

**¿Jugar sobre seguro es la respuesta?** La pregunta es: ¿hasta qué punto es mucho más seguro proseguir en una esfera acomodaticia? Todos sabemos que los cambios efectivos pueden desestimarse ante las docenas de proyectos que se amontonan en los escritorios de los gestores, de modo que se imponga una mentalidad corta de miras y tendente a la inercia. Cuando los riesgos para hacerse con una campaña o lanzar un nuevo producto son elevados, la tendencia suele ser el recurso a lo que fuera que funcionó la última vez. Antes las pretensiones de los accionistas y en un apurado entorno económico, el balance final o incluso la mera supervivencia pasan a ser la prioridad máxima: a los que asumen riesgos se les suele mostrar la salida. A corto plazo, esta limitada estrategia puede permitir que la compañía vaya tirando. Los empleados brindarán los mismos resultados de siempre con regularidad robótica, sin inspiración ni nuevos esquemas. Y la creatividad se estancará enseguida. «Siempre se ha hecho así» y «No hay tiempo para más» pasan a ser los mantras.

**El cambio es capacitación.** De hecho, hacer las cosas de otro modo –un modo más estimulante y abierto a territorios inexplorados- es la esencia del cambio. En el proceso hallaremos nuevos y provechosos estímulos que, en el contexto adecuado, pueden propulsar rápidamente un negocio. El cambio es el más poderoso factor de motivación para empleados y propietarios: es aquello que separa el estancamiento de la excelencia.

*Relogo* trata justamente de esos cambios. Celebramos la chispa de una idea que vibra en la imaginación de alguien para convertirse en llamarada. Nos mueve la auténtica diferencia y las identidades poderosas que hacen descollar a estas marcas. Abrazamos también las nuevas tecnologías a fin de que el consumidor comprenda mejor su funcionamiento y todo aquello en torno a lo que el mundo gira. En estas páginas, encontrará estimulantes maneras para consumar los cambios e información detallada acerca de lo que significa mantenerse vivo y alerta: la capacidad de vestir con «hábitos» nuevos la identidad de una marca.

En definitiva, espero que la lectura de *Relogo* represente un viaje apasionante hacia la novedad –y el abandono de lo caduco-, embarcados en la aventura de identidades corporativas revitalizadas: marcas que asumieron cambios pequeños, medianos o grandes, pero siempre significativos.

Hasta pronto: a por los cambios.

# El logotipo no basta para crear una identidad de marca

Joe Duffy
Presidente de Duffy & Partners

El primer logotipo se diseñó a finales del siglo XIX.

Durante 30 años, yo me he dedicado a crear identidades de marca, de modo que quizá resulte curioso oírme decir que la mayor parte del mundo del diseño concede una importancia excesiva al logotipo. Es más, considero que está sobredimensionado. Por mucho que admire la destilación de la esencia de una marca en un simple emblema gráfico, debo decir que incluso cuando se hace de modo eficaz (algo más bien raro, por cierto), su resultado no deja de ser una de las muchas «piezas móviles» destinadas a crear una conexión entre la marca y el público al que se orienta.

Lo que una marca exitosa necesita es un «lenguaje» completo, que resulte único y relevante para su público y del que éste pueda apropiarse. Este lenguaje debe ser, como mínimo, tridimensional. Debería ponderar cómo se ve, suena y se siente dicha marca, e incluso cómo huele y a qué sabe. Debe comunicar, honestamente, por qué existe y en qué sentido la aprueban sus usuarios. El lenguaje de marca no es una mera cuestión de marketing, balances comerciales o consumismo, sino que supone una invitación a sumarse a una causa. Y, francamente, es imposible que un logotipo cumpla con todo ese cometido.

El logo es el eje en torno al cual gira el lenguaje de marca. Es una suerte de firma que debería vincularse a los rasgos de la «persona» que la ejecuta. Su apariencia puede ser un comienzo, pero la cosa no termina ahí. Si proseguimos con la analogía personal, las características del logo y su lenguaje de marca complementario deben configurar un sistema de creencias y hacerlo con un estilo particular –del mismo modo en que la gente se viste o comparte sus ideas–, que atraiga a todas aquellas personas que sientan afinidad por cosas parecidas.

Si los diseñadores aspiran a registrar un auténtico impacto económico con el diseño de marca, deben trascender la dimensión del mero logo. En mi opinión, el proceso creativo que nos atañe no debería comenzar ni finalizar con el logo. Debería iniciarse a partir de la observación: la curiosidad es lo que nos permite ver las cosas de otro modo. El proceso creativo consiste tanto en cuestionar la historia de la marca y de cultura de quienes están detrás de sus productos y servicios, en comprender su medio de competencia y el lugar que ocupa en las vidas de las personas, como en la creación de nuevos recursos visuales. Y consiste en estar culturalmente despierto y saber cómo subsiste una marca en el mundo.

Lo he presenciado incontables veces: un diseñador atiende a su inclinación primera de desmantelar una identidad existente para acometer de la nada un nuevo diseño de logo. Me parece una actitud algo ególatra. Existe un enfoque más respetuoso y sensible: estudiar el pasado. Esto es, analizar el bagaje negativo de su herencia e identidad, así como el legado positivo, y atacar el proyecto desde ahí.

A lo largo de los años, parte de nuestro más logrado trabajo de identidad corporativa se ha acometido con empresas cuyo logo se dejó intacto, o quizá se retocó levemente, se reavivó, revitalizándolo. Los diseñadores siempre deseamos provocar cierto impacto, queremos dejar huella. Nuestros clientes y socios empresariales aspiran a eso mismo. En tal sentido, en nuestro trabajo de diseño de logos y desarrollo de lenguajes de marca, debemos considerar al logo como un elemento más. El logo es como la firma: significativa, personal y única. Al igual que su creador, debe evolucionar con el tiempo, y todos los cambios deberían reflejar el lugar que ocupa en el ámbito más amplio de la comunidad y la cultura a las que pertenece.

Creo firmemente que los mejores diseñadores se dedican a estudiar detenidamente la cultura, las tendencias y las artes y oficios relacionados. En ese sentido, este libro debe jugar su papel en vuestros estudios acerca de los logotipos: cuántos se crean y evolucionan, su rol en el lenguaje de marca y en la creación de identidades corporativas que superan la prueba del tiempo de modo relevante y duradero.

# Rediseñar el logo

Wu Qiaohui
Director editorial

El logotipo es el agente visual de la marca. Nike se asocia de inmediato con una tilde invertida, Apple con una manzana mordida y Chanel con dos "C" simétricas entrelazadas. Al hablar de una marca determinada, la gente imagina enseguida su logo. Ésa es precisamente la función de identidad visual del logo. De hecho, el logo y la marca se complementan. Un logo excelente otorga a la marca una imagen visual única, y viceversa, el éxito de una marca mejora la percepción del logo.

En años recientes, los progresos, la evolución de las tendencias y la competición enconada han llevado a las marcas a plantearse el rediseño de sus logos. Un logo nuevo juega un rol fundamental a la hora de fijar una clientela nueva, promocionar la marca y elevar su prestigio, con lo cual toda un serie de aspectos visuales vinculados a la marca deben concebirse de nuevo a partir del logo.

Rediseñar el logo tiene sus riesgos. Un diseño de logo excelente que goce de buena aceptación puede favorecer a la marca. Sin embargo, si el logo nuevo no recaba la aceptación del público debido a la arraigada impresión que el antiguo ejerce sobre él, no sólo toparemos con críticas al nuevo diseño, sino que la propia marca se hallará inmersa en un conflicto. En comparación con el diseño de un logo nuevo, rediseñar otro ya existente se antoja más complicado. Para obtener la aprobación del público, el nuevo logo debe superar la popularidad del anterior por medio de una solución radical y sorpresiva que se convierta en una experiencia visual de marca completamente nueva.

Existen tres vías para el desarrollo de proyectos destinados a rediseñar un logo. La primera consiste en rediseñar el logo preservando ciertos elementos del anterior, tales como color, forma, tipo de letra, etc. La segunda pasa por romper las limitaciones del viejo logo y dar con uno completamente diferente a fin de presentar nuevas posibilidades a la marca. La tercera consiste en crear una serie de logos que son, en esencia, el mismo, pero exhiben aspectos cambiantes. La variabilidad y la flexibilidad son factores que pueden expresar bien el vigor y la vitalidad de la marca y sus diversas facetas.

La calidad del diseño del logo en sí mismo es un criterio determinante para juzgarlo. Pero tras años de evolución y desarrollo, actualmente el diseño del logo no se limita a éste, sino que implica el de otras aplicaciones que lo complementan. Algunos diseños de logos son sobresalientes en sí mismos al reflejar las características de la marca, expresar su filosofía empresarial y captar la atención del público; en tanto que otros son menos impactantes, pero con la suma de esas otras aplicaciones pueden, a la postre, obtener el mismo efecto.

Además de exhibir numerosos trabajos en el diseño de logos, *Relogo* debate los desafíos a que se enfrentan las marcas, las dificultades con que deben lidiar los diseñadores y el resultado obtenido por los logos rediseñados, mediante la inclusión de sugerencias por parte de los clientes y de la filosofía sobre el diseño que ofrecen diversas agencias. Los lectores pueden así comprender la historia detrás de la marca, y obtener fuentes de inspiración abundantes y valiosas.

# :PREFAZIONE

## Dal vecchio al nuovo - come le cose devono cambiare

Gion-Men Kruegel-Hanna
Direttore Esecutivo Creativo di Interbrand

Benvenuti in *Relogo*, una meravigliosa pubblicazione che celebra il nuovo e il vecchio insieme. Ciascuna delle storie in questo libro ci accompagna in un viaggio attraverso la rivitalizzazione di un'azienda, un servizio, un prodotto o un marchio a noi caro, quale che sia la nostra provenienza. I casi presentati in queste pagine hanno tutti due cose in comune: portano con sé un'eredità dal passato e hanno attraversato un qualche tipo di cambiamento, magari solo un ritocco sottile ma importante all'identità visuale, o anche una completa ri-creazione del logo.

**Uno sguardo intorno a noi.** Prima di occuparci a fondo del significato di "cambiamento" per un marchio in termini di forma, attitudine, natura e poteri, è senz'altro il caso di notare che il mondo in cui viviamo si trova in uno stato di flusso e movimento costante. Allo stesso tempo, la nostra natura di esseri umani tende a farci sentire a nostro agio con ciò che ci è familiare e abbiamo imparato a conoscere e apprezzare. Eppure, anche sulla spinta della globalizzazione e della presenza sempre maggiore della tecnologia nelle nostre vite, ci dobbiamo adattare a un mondo in rapido cambiamento.

Pensando alle aziende rappresentate in questo libro, siano esse piccole imprese a conduzione familiare o grosse società multinazionali, per tutte loro ci sono voluti parecchi anni per consolidare i propri valori, attraverso il modo di operare ma anche grazie all'aspetto dell'azienda e alle sensazioni che essa suscita. Vale lo stesso per il tono di voce: il modo in cui una marca si esprime, informa e si rivolge al proprio pubblico e ai propri clienti riguardo ai prodotti e ai servizi che offre ha la stessa importanza. Per di più, molte di queste aziende hanno instaurato relazioni a lungo termine attraverso i rapporti con i clienti e l'espansione del portafoglio prodotti. Dal piccolo bar di quartiere all'identità di una città intera, queste organizzazioni hanno anche saputo incoraggiare il loro personale a guardare oltre i compiti primordiali e scoprire aree più ampie ed estese, con un pubblico più vasto con il quale trattare.

Inoltre, molte di queste aziende hanno investito fortemente nell'immagine del loro marchio e del loro disegno, comprendendo che l'identità del marchio non è un male necessario (ossia qualcosa in cui non si vorrebbe veramente investire, ma che alla fine si deve curare solo perché lo fanno tutti gli altri). Al contrario, tutti ormai si sono resi conto che un'identità che si distingua dalle altre è un must per chi si vuole affermare, per chi vuole farsi vedere e sentire e per chi vuole fare affari migliori e più consistenti con più clienti. E tutto ciò aggiunge ulteriore valore al business.

**Il percorso del cambiamento.** Sarà anche vero che il cambiamento è il cammino più spaventoso tra tutti quelli che si possono scegliere, ma di certo è un aspetto essenziale nel mondo d'oggi a cento all'ora e un fattore cruciale per un futuro sostenibile, e inoltre la buona salute e la crescita continua dei nostri marchi favoriti dipendono da questo tipo di progresso. È per questo che possiamo viaggiare in automobile anziché in una carrozza a cavalli e inviare rapidi messaggini senza dover cercare un telefono a gettoni. Il cambiamento ha influito pesantemente anche sul modo in cui ci muoviamo per il mondo, sulle nostre modalità di accesso a ciò di cui abbiamo bisogno per la nostra felicità quotidiana e su come guardiamo, ascoltiamo e annusiamo nuove culture prima sconosciute.

A dire il vero, si potrebbe forse sostenere che il cambiamento e la globalizzazione ci hanno presentato molte sfide a volte ardue da affrontare o anche solo da comprendere. Eppure, in egual misura, oggi "cambiamento" significa che se a qualcuno cade uno spillo nell'angolo più remoto della terra saremo in grado di sentirne il rumore all'istante, ovunque ci troviamo. Che ci piaccia o no, così vanno le cose, e allora guardiamole dal lato buono e afferriamo le opportunità che si presentano davanti a noi.

Soluzione: evitare i rischi? A questo punto, la domanda cruciale è la seguente: rimanere al riparo all'interno della nostra "zona di comodità" è davvero così sicuro? Tutti noi sappiamo bene che un cambiamento positivo può finire nel cestino nel momento i cui i manager hanno decine di progetti che si accumulano sulla scrivania. Una mentalità da catena di montaggio, o con il paraocchi, può imporsi facilmente. Quando la posta in gioco è importante nella conquista di nuovi mercati o nel lancio di un nuovo prodotto, la tentazione è quella di sputare fuori, tale e quale, la soluzione che ha funzionato l'ultima volta. Quando gli azionisti reclamano, le necessità di base o anche semplicemente la sopravvivenza assumono la massima priorità in ambienti economici difficili, e a quel punto non c'è più spazio per che ama il rischio. Nel breve termine questa strategia limitata può anche permettere all'azienda di barcamenarsi in qualche modo, e i dipendenti continueranno a produrre lo stesso risultato, in maniera quasi robotica, senza ispirazione né rinnovate motivazioni. Ma presto la creatività ristagna. I nuovi mantra diventeranno "abbiamo sempre fatto così" e "non abbiamo abbastanza tempo".

**Il cambiamento è potere.** Viceversa, agire in modo diverso, ossia in una maniera più ispirata, scoprendo nuovi territori, è l'essenza del cambiamento. Lungo il cammino possiamo trovare nuovi stimoli, fruttuosi ed eccitanti, che inquadrati nel giusto contesto possono dare una forte spinta in avanti a un'azienda. Il cambiamento è il singolo fattore motivante più potente tra i dipendenti e per i proprietari della marca, ed è ciò che distingue la stagnazione dall'eccellenza.

Questo è il cambiamento che *Relogo* ha in mente, celebrando il modo in cui il primo barlume di un'idea, una scintilla nell'immaginazione di qualcuno, può accendere una fiamma radiante. Da qui nasce la vera distinzione, e i marchi in grado di costruirsi una forte identità sono quelli che spiccano. Si tratterà anche di abbracciare nuove tecnologie e trasmettere ai clienti una migliore comprensione su ciò che succede intorno a loro e su cosa fa girare il mondo. In queste pagine troverete nuove modalità e nuove fonti di ispirazione per arrivare al cambiamento, informazioni approfondite sul significato di una mente aperta e vivace e suggerimenti su come si può "vestire a nuovo" l'identità di una marca.

Per concludere, mi auguro che la lettura di *Relogo* vi accompagni in un viaggio stimolante, abbracciando il nuovo e lasciando il vecchio dietro di voi per imbarcarvi in un'avventura fatta di identità di marca rivitalizzate, tutte uscite da un cambiamento, piccolo, moderato o grande, ma comunque importante.

Buon viaggio – sulle ali del cambiamento.

# Non basta un logo per costruire l'identità di una marca

Joe Duffy
Presidente di Duffy & Partners

Il primo logo è stato disegnato, da qualche parte, verso la fine del 1800. Personalmente creo nuove identità di marca da oltre 30 anni, perciò forse suonerà strano se sostengo che la maggior parte di coloro che operano nel campo del design infila troppa roba nei "logo" – davvero troppa. Anzi, credo che l'importanza del logo sia sopravvalutata. Per quanto possa apprezzare la distillazione dell'essenza di una marca in una semplice rappresentazione grafica, anche nei casi in cui viene eseguita correttamente (rari, a dire il vero), questa operazione non è che uno degli ingranaggi del meccanismo in grado di creare un collegamento riuscito tra una marca e il pubblico al quale essa è destinata.

Ciò di cui le marche di successo hanno bisogno è un intero "linguaggio": una lingua unica, possedibile e importante per le persone a cui si tiene di più. Dovrà essere un linguaggio tridimensionale e anche più, dovendo tenere conto del modo in cui la marca viene vista, sentita e toccata, e magari anche annusata e assaggiata. Dovrà trasmettere in tutta onestà il motivo per il quale la marca esiste ed è adatta a chi ne fa parte. Il linguaggio di una marca è un invito al pubblico a partecipare a una causa, almeno tanto quanto è marketing, affari o consumismo. Francamente, ottenere tutto questo con un semplice logo è impossibile.

Pensate al logo come al fulcro attorno al quale il linguaggio della marca ruota. Essendo una sorta di firma, dovrebbe rappresentare le caratteristiche della "persona" che la appone. Il look può essere il punto di partenza, ma non finisce certo lì. Rimanendo nell'analogia della persona, le caratteristiche del logo e il più completo linguaggio della marca saranno lo specchio di ciò in cui si crede e dovranno raccontare la storia di uno stile particolare, così come una persona si vestirebbe o condividerebbe le proprie idee, coinvolgendo gli amici e chiunque si senta attratto da questo genere di cose nel corso del processo.

Se un designer vuole lasciare un segno reale e tangibile sugli affari di una marca con un nuovo design, dovrà pensare oltre il logo. A mio parere il processo creativo non inizia né finisce con il logo. In realtà dovrebbe iniziare con l'osservazione: è la curiosità che ci fa vedere le cose in un modo nuovo. Il processo creativo consiste nel porsi domande sulla storia di una marca e sulla cultura delle persone che stanno dietro i suoi prodotti e servizi, comprendendo la situazione rispetto alla concorrenza e il posto occupato dalla marca nella vita delle persone, almeno tanto quanto consiste nella pura creazione di rappresentazioni grafiche. In un senso ancora più importante, si tratta di essere consapevoli della cultura della marca e di come essa viva il suo mondo.

Troppe volte ho visto designer rimanere fedeli alla tendenza immediata a smantellare un'identità esistente e partire con un nuovo logo da zero. Direi che questo è il trionfo dell'ego. L'approccio più rispettoso e appropriato consiste nello studiare ciò che è stato fatto in passato, analizzando il patrimonio ereditario e identificando i retaggi negativi, insieme con i valori positivi, per poi costruire a partire da questo punto.

In tutti questi anni, parte del nostro lavoro più riuscito sull'identità di marca riguarda casi in cui il logo preesistente è stato lasciato intatto o magari sviluppato, rinfrescato o rivitalizzato. Come designer, tutti noi vogliamo lasciare il segno, desideriamo lasciare qualcosa dietro di noi, e i nostri clienti e partner in affari vogliono lo stesso. Così, mentre ci diamo da fare per disegnare nuovi logo e sviluppare linguaggi di marca per creare identità di marca significative, dobbiamo ricordare che il logo, nel suo ruolo, non è che tra i tanti elementi. Il logo è come una firma: importante, personale e unica. Così come colui che la appone, la firma stessa può evolvere nel tempo, ma ogni eventuale cambiamento dovrà riflettere il suo posto nel contesto della comunità e l'ampiezza della cultura in cui essa esiste.

Ritengo che i migliori designer siano in realtà studenti della cultura, delle tendenze e del loro stesso mestiere. In questa ottica, il libro che avete in mano può giocare un ruolo fondamentale nei vostri studi sui logo, su come molti di essi vengono creati e si evolvono e sul loro ruolo nei linguaggi di marca e nella creazione di identità di marca che sappiano superare la prova del tempo trasmettendo un significato e lasciando un segno.

# Logo Remake

Wu Qiaohui
Executive Editor

Il logo è il rappresentante visuale della marca: associamo immediatamente Nike con un baffo, Apple con una mela morsicata e Chanel con due lettere C simmetriche e intrecciate tra loro. Quando parliamo di una certa marca, nella mente delle persone appare il suo logo. È questa la funzione di identificazione globale del logo. Anzi, si può dire che il logo e la marca si completano tra loro. Un grande logo assicura a una marca un'immagine visuale unica, e viceversa il successo di una marca eleva la connotazione del suo logo.

I tempi cambiano, le tendenze evolvono e la concorrenza è feroce: tutto questo ha stimolato parecchie case a ricorrere al ridisegno del proprio logo negli ultimi anni, con il nuovo logo che giocherà un luogo fondamentale nella ridefinizione del target di clienti, promuovendo la marca, aumentandone il prestigio e inducendo una riprogettazione sistematica dell'immagine visiva della marca, da centrare attorno al nuovo logo.

Per ridisegnare un logo è necessario prendere dei rischi. Se un disegno eccellente e ampiamente accettato può portare benefici alla marca, un nuovo logo non accettato dal pubblico (probabilmente a causa di una radicata abitudine per quello vecchio) non solo susciterà critiche sul nuovo logo, ma farà sorgere anche dei dubbi sulla marca stessa. Rispetto al disegno di un logo nuovo di zecca per una marca, il ridisegno di un logo esistente appare più complicato. Per ottenere l'approvazione da parte del pubblico, il nuovo logo dovrà raggiungere e superare il successo di quello vecchio e generare elementi di sorpresa e innovazione, creando così una nuova esperienza visuale per la marca.

Esistono tre tipi di percorsi di sviluppo per i vari progetti di ridisegno del logo. Il primo percorso è il ridisegno sulla base "ereditaria" di una parte degli elementi del vecchio logo, quali il colore, la forma, il carattere di stampa e così via. Il secondo percorso consiste nel rompere completamente i limiti del vecchio logo applicando un disegno completamente diverso, in modo da aprire la marca a nuove potenziali possibilità. Il terzo percorso prevede la creazione di una serie di modelli di logo simili ma con sfaccettature diverse. La modificabilità e la flessibilità possono esprimere al meglio il vigore e la vitalità del marchio e i suoi diversi aspetti.

La qualità del disegno stesso del logo è un criterio assai importante per giudicare il logo. Dopo anni di evoluzione e sviluppo, il design di un nuovo logo non sarà confinato nei limiti del logo, ma richiederà ulteriori elementi di application design che vanno oltre il logo stesso. In certi casi il disegno del logo è straordinario di per sé, riflettendo le caratteristiche della marca, elaborando la sua filosofia di gestione e catturando gli sguardi del pubblico, mentre in altri casi il logo, pur non essendo altrettanto impressionante, può ottenere lo stesso effetto se abbinato ad altri aspetti di application design.

Oltre a presentare un gran numero di casi reali, *Relogo* discute le sfide che la marca si trova a dover affrontare e le difficoltà in cui incappano i designer dovendo tenere conto dei suggerimenti dei clienti e dell'influenza delle filosofie grafico-progettuali seguite dall'agenzia di design. I lettori potranno comprendere le storie che stanno dietro le marche e attingere a un'abbondante e preziosa fonte di informazioni.

# :CONTENTS

## :PREFACE
Pages 004 - 019

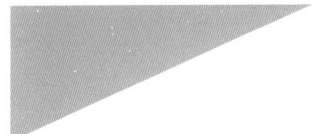

## :OVERTURN
Pages 126 - 225

## :WORK INDEX
Pages 268 - 271

## :ACKNOWLEDGEMENTS
Pages 272

## :SIMILAR DIFFERENCE
Pages 022 - 125

## :DIVERSITY
Pages 226 - 261

## :DESIGNER INDEX
Pages 264 - 267

:Similar Difference

01 AÏSHTI

01

Brand identity for AÏSHTI, a Beirut-based luxury retailer with store locations throughout the Middle East. This identity includes the parent AÏSHTI brand, as well as its young adult brand AÏZONE and its children's brand AÏSHTI Minis.

The identity includes design for all three brands' stationery sets, primary collateral and store materials. Additionally, the brand identity was extended via the seasonal print campaigns that appeared in newspapers, magazines, and billboards throughout Lebanon.

:Similar Difference

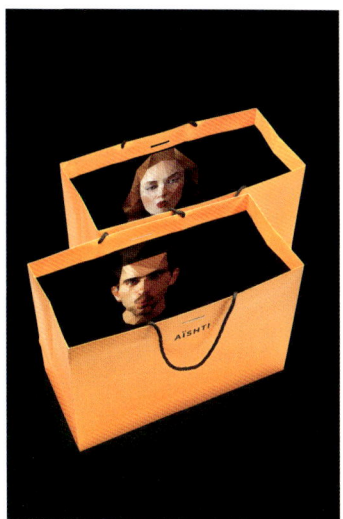

:Similar Difference

02 BMJ Architects

03 ÒMNIUM llengua Cultura País

04 Rosendahl

**02**
**:Client's Brief**
BMJ Architects wanted to redesign the existing logotype, brand identity guidelines and website.

**:Design Philosophy**
El Studio redesigned the logotype to reflect the modern approach BMJ Architects apply to design. The brand guidelines were designed to maintain consistency of the brand throughout the 4 offices in the United Kingdom.

**03**
**:Client's Brief**
ÒMNIUM llengua Cultura País asked for branding redesign to renew it without losing the "historical values".

**:Design Philosophy**
"OMNIUM" logo was simplified and the assignment of a "Catalan" color (Yellow-red-orange).

**04**
**:Client's Brief**
Rosendahl wanted to refresh their products' image to appeal to contemporary tastes yet, with more than 400 different products on the shelves, needed to introduce an identity that can live alongside the old.

**:Design Philosophy**
The new design retains its predecessor's elegance yet is warmer and more contemporary. The new identity is currently living alongside their older packaging and drawing a new generation to the Rosendahl brand.

## 05 ArtComArt

ArtComArt is a press photography agency rich of 25 years of archives devoted to all the arts. Pascal Victor and Victor Tonelli, photographers, have entrusted Murmure for the creation of their visual identity and the realization of their website.

The identity is based on black to symbolize photography and a deep red as for the velvet of theater seats. The business card is simple, mostly black. The logo is red and the "o" at the center of the logotype is highlighted by an opacity game with the names written on the back. Murmure also designed letterheads and the greeting card. Presented in a fancy envelope, folded and sealed by a red velvet sticker they have a detachable business card on one side.

For the website, the objective was to create a simple presentation, focusing on photography and the notions of service and art. A simple search system, efficient and fluid, has been established to allow press agencies to quickly find among the 200,000 referenced images, the one expected, by directors, places, or actors.

:Similar Difference

06 JWI Louvres

06
:Client's Brief
JWI Louvres briefed their redesign with three powerful words: "bold, simple, modern." Working frequently with architects and designers, the company needed an identity that spoke to a visually literate audience and, if possible, reflected the products they produce.

:Design Philosophy
The resulting identity plays with louvres in a dynamic and engaging way. The lines reposition on each piece of collateral, effectively opening or closing depending on the application. With a refreshed palette of bright red and deep black foil, JWI Louvres' new identity thoroughly delivers on "bold, simple and modern".

:Similar Difference

07 IPMARK

08 SVEDKA

09 SUSO

07
:Client's Brief
IPMARK is a leading marketing magazine in Spain. They needed to revamp the identity, without adding too much noise.

:Design Philosophy
Clean new identity was created, stressing the essence of the brand, with no intention of adding anything unnecessary.

08
As one of America's top 5 vodka brands, the aim was to create a higher level of visibility and sophistication on premise as its targeted area for growth, while maintaining its robust business on the mass market.

09
:Client's Brief
The aim was to develop the identity and visual language for a carbonated fruit juice with no preservatives or additives and which was targeting a young audience in the UK market; the new logo was meant to express the "natural" and "social" character of the brand.

:Design Philosophy
The original Helvetica was slightly modified to fit with the new design, an asterisk was created to express the two brand values: its leafy shapes are reminiscent of nature, while the 5 parts of which it is composed are to evoke the feeling of sharing and coming together.

:Similar Difference

10 The PURE Water Co.

# THE PURE WATER C⁰

# PURE.

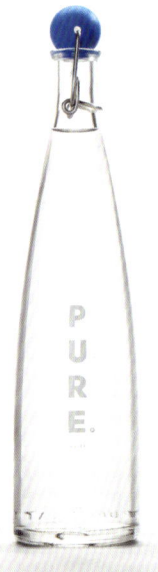

10
:Client's Brief
The PURE Water Co. wanted to redesign their identity to convey the environmental and health benefits of their product, while maintaining their focus on innovation and design.

:Design Philosophy
The characters were redrawn to work both horizontally for the company identity and vertically for the product brand, while the color and shape of the registered trademark links the well known bottle cap, the communication concept and the logo all together.

:Similar Difference

:Similar Difference

11 Spudbar

11
Spudbar was founded in Melbourne in 2000, born out of a frustration at the lack of a healthy, great tasting feed that was quick, convenient and value for money. It has been on a mission from day one to create a new category of food offer that fuses natural goodness and big flavours into the nutrient rich gem that is the steaming baked spud.

When Truly Deeply began working with Spudbar they had 9 stores around Australia and were struggling to own a space in the market compelling enough to grow the business to the next level.

Truly Deeply immersed themselves in Spudbar's market segment, generated some clear qualitative market insights, and led a brand strategy rethink to provide a clear vision for where the brand and its offer could most potently be positioned for success in the market.

The key to developing the Spudbar brand identity and retail environment to match the newly defined brand proposition was all about unlocking the visual cues of the classic, one-off local cafe. By unlocking the code of visual language for these unique, high-loyalty, non-franchise food businesses, Truly Deeply developed the Spudbar brand identity to work in a similar, non-cookie cutter manner.

:Similar Difference

:Similar Difference

## [12] Little Chef

Little Chef roadside restaurants have been a British institution for over 50 years. But in recent years, as travelers' needs changed, Little Chef didn't. It lost its place as the nation's favorite place to stop, replaced by the likes of McDonalds, M&S, and branded service stations.

venturethree repositioned the brand as "Wonderfully British", bringing the food, service, environment and communications together under one strong brand. The positioning underpins every area of the business, giving Little Chef a rich territory to own. With freshly cooked food, made just for you, Little Chef is more relevant today than ever.

venturethree created a powerful look and feel that establishes Little Chef as a thoroughly modern British brand, allowing them to sit confidently alongside the competition. They developed an internal and external signage system, new menus, and packaging for the new Good to Go range. The cheeky new tone-of-voice sounds individual and independent, not corporate and consistent. venturethree retained and updated original elements of the brand, giving Charlie, Little Chef's iconic brand symbol, a makeover to give him new energy and purpose.

The new Little Chef is fresh, fun and Wonderfully British. The best place to stop, whatever your journey.

:Similar Difference

13 MARTINS

14 Caras Gourmet

15 Jack in the Box

13
:Client's Brief
MARTINS is a restaurant, whose target was mostly woman between 30 and 50 years, but now they want to get young people attention.

:Design Philosophy
MANIFIESTO FUTURA had the instruction of keeping the simbol of the heart; they use strong typography, with a mix of a delicate but strong icon to get a younger target.

14
:Client's Brief
Caras Gourmet asked for redesigning their existing logo. Create a clean, simple solution that they can apply to all their products without loosing the essence of their corporate identity.

:Design Philosophy
Floor5 decided to extract the most interesting element from the old logo, which is the lady with a cup on her head and concentrated on it as the main motive. They got rid of details such as body, beans, steam and color and created a logo which was simple and easy to read without loosing the resemblance to the original. The silhouette of a lady with a cup on her head was created.

15
The new primary brand identity for Jack in the Box restaurants was designed to put a fresh face on an old friend. Acknowledging consumers' verbal short hand and their love of the fictional CEO featured in the brand's marketing campaign, the mark shortens the name to Jack. The simple script type was chosen to reflect the casual, fun-loving personal signature of the man behind the brand.

:Similar Difference

### 16   The Marmalade Pantry

:Similar Difference

The Marmalade Pantry is a popular and upmarket café that prides itself on offering "good things to eat". As the restaurant was moving to its new premises at Singapore's premier shopping gallery – the Ion Orchard – in August 2009, the management decided to embark on a rebranding exercise to establish a new look, by way of refreshing its identity and the restaurant collaterals.

The brief was open but simple: the new logo needs to incorporate some elements of the old, in order to not alienate the consumers from what was already established. Also, a decidedly more mature and classier approach would be befitting of its relocation to Ion Orchard, home also to a number of premium fashion boutiques.

As such, &Larry worked closely with the client and interior designer to create an organic and memorable identity to go hand-in-hand with the branding and environment.

The minimalist, even austere, approach was a deliberate decision as &Larry wanted to differentiate from the usual pastel-shaded and prettily detailed boutique cake shops and cafés that were in direct competition with their client.

The custom logotype is placed within a silhouette that coincides with any number of "good things to eat": fresh baked breads, cupcakes, fruits, cheeses, vegetables and meats, etc.

The logomark is applied consistently across the full range of stationery and store collaterals, including store cards, place mats, etc.

Collaterals for use within the restaurant included a multipurpose sticker which was created to label boxes and take-out packaging, as well as a custom-made cloth-bound menu board. The menu board features slip-in pockets to hold an A3 sheet, which is designed for easy updating by the client with standard office software. The board itself underwent testing to withstand the casual stacking and handling that comes with daily use.

The café signage was designed around several building limitations. As wiring could only come through the ceiling, the solution was to mount the sign on the cross section of a hollow pillar. The arrangement allowed the distinctive sign to be lit and visible from the major directions of foot traffic approaching the café.

A series of press advertisements was created to coincide with the launch of the new flagship café. Each featured a clean, minimalist photograph of a key ingredient for one of the signature dishes on the menu. The purity and goodness of the foods come across directly to whet readers' appetites. The Marmalade Pantry mark is always stamped front and centre to claim ownership of this branding trait.

:Similar Difference

17 OIC

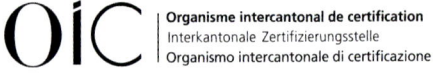 

 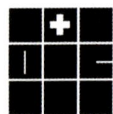    

17
:Client's Brief
OIC is a simple Swiss certification. Created by agreement signed between the cantons of Bern, Fribourg, Ticino, Vaud, Valais, Neuchâtel, Geneva and Jura, it provides certification for food manufacturers wishing to obtain a distinctive sign that will bring recognition and protection to their specialty.

:Design Philosophy
Keeping the setting of the previous logo, Blackswan applied red which is the color of Swiss national flag as the theme color of the new logo. The white cross in the letter "O" resembled that in the national flag as well.

18 Anboto

19 Iskon Broadband Telecom

20 Fibrelac

18
:Client's Brief
Anboto is a local Basque newspaper. They asked di-da komunikakzioa (communication) to redesign their logo.

:Design Philosophy
A updated logo which also maintained the key element of the previous logo was created.

19
:Client's Brief
Iskon were the first company to bring broadband to Croatia, however they hadn't rebranded since their launch and asked for a face-lift.

:Design Philosophy
Bunch maintained the integrity and heritage of the brand but managed to drastically update the image of the company.

20
:Client's Brief
Fibrelac is the pioneer in fiber optic networks in Switzerland. Fibrelac had grown much faster than its brand identity which remained that of a startup.

:Design Philosophy
A new logo and a brand new universe that is coherent, original and vocational gave an image to its measure "national dynamic, highly skilled".

:Similar Difference

21 Calango

22 UniGEO

23 Niko

21
:Client's Brief
After a few years of designing for clients, Calango thought that it was time to redesign their logo as well. The brief was to keep things typographic and clean, while being less trendy than the original one.

:Design Philosophy
Together with intern Sandra Gutkin, Calango heavily customized Times New Romand Bold, in order to get a unique and timeless look.

22
:Client's Brief
The aim was to create a new visual identity for this newly established e-learning company, and help them hunt down their first clients.

:Design Philosophy
The solution was to create a logotype full of gravitas and solidity. To give this new company a more trustwurthy look. And to create a strong visual link between the company UniGEO and the product GEOClass.

23
:Client's Brief
The image of Niko, Belgium's leading electric switches and domotics brand with a strong presence throughout Europe, needed to evolve from a manufacturer to a solutions provider on lighting, access, energy and safety.

:Design Philosophy
Whilst respecting the traditional value of Niko's long history, the new logo reflects Niko's reliability as well as its innovative approach, presenting a brand identity that is well-balanced, rich in light and colour.

:Similar Difference

24 Dasko

25 Fallen

26 Sati

24
:Client's Brief
Dasko, a family-owned auto-electrical parts business, asked Everything Design to help them reposition and refresh the company brand and enhance the appeal and effectiveness of their marketing communications, both in print and online.

:Design Philosophy
Everything Design saw the obvious opportunity to simplify the company's brand architecture which was overly complicated and had diluted brand recognition and understanding as a consequence. With a much simpler system in place, they then refined the original brand identity to give it a stronger visual presence and make it much more robust in application.

25
:Client's Brief
The objective was to redesign the band logo, try to avoid clichés such as the use of distorted, horrormovie-like gothic letters, make it more compromiseless and self-conscient.

:Design Philosophy
As metal bands mostly communicate very pronounced ideas and visions on the world, using straight-forward and to-the-point lyrics, it seemed like an obvious choice not to distort the self-made font, in order to achieve a rather steadvast, fine-tuned and sharp-edged logo.

26
:Client's Brief
The aim was to redesign the Sati company logo, make it feel less static and visually more connected with the core business, rolling stock maintenance.

:Design Philosophy
The former logo didn't have too much breathing space and felt kind of aggressive, Raf Vancampenhoudt wanted to create more openness, make the company look more human and dynamic, which is suggested by an opened circular form combined with a diagonal dynamic suggesting a rolling movement.

:Similar Difference

27 Wanjia Media Group

28 Iboardcast

29 Palm

27
:Client's Brief
MetaDesign was entrusted with the repositioning of the Group and its magazines, which called for redesign at many levels. A shift in business priorities had necessitated this corporate identity change.

:Design Philosophy
The catalyst of happiness: Life is made up of precious moments that are sometimes hard to see. Wanjia highlights the beautiful facets of life, adds color, enjoyment and substance to every moment, opens up your eyes and mind. Facets like these become the catalyst of an even greater, happier life.

28
El Miro updated the logo of Iboardcast, and make it cool. He thought that the old logo was not so good for using.

29
:Client's Brief
Palm won back its brand from the software division and sought to recapture the spirit of its original logo (also designed by Turner Duckworth in 1999), while signaling a positive change.

:Design Philosophy
The original Palm logo was designed to express simplicity and delight – the characteristics shared by all Palm products. The update to orange communicated the brand's commitment to innovation, while the pixel inspired redrawn type gave the word mark a modern feeling and allowed it to stand on its own outside the medallion.

:Similar Difference

30 Probst

31 Globull

32 Dolby

30
:Client's Brief
A complete redesign regardless existing, reducing the company name to Probst.

:Design Philosophy
The custom cut letters give the brand a strong, distinctive identity and fit the furniture and design sector.

31
:Client's Brief
Globull asked for redesigning the club identity while keeping the pure fonts line and adding a visual grip with the letters abbreviation "G".

:Design Philosophy
Inventaire wanted to draw and create a more pure font and rework the whole identity to be more homogeneous.

32
:Client's Brief
Join together Dolby's two unique places in the industry: as an ingredient brand in some instances and a marquee brand in others.

:Design Philosophy
Turner Duckworth revised the "Double D" speakers to make the icon more expressive and iconic, and created foundational elements such as photography style, graphic layouts, new graphic devices, color and typography. The visual identity design was applied across multiple brand activations that bring the brand to life in an engaging and imaginative way.

:Similar Difference

33 DJ Will Clarke

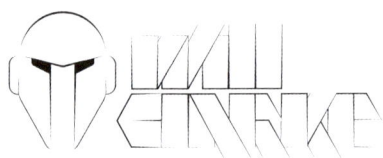

33
:Client's Brief
Will Clarke had seen one of Superfried's robot characters and commissioned them to create one to represent him.

:Design Philosophy
Superfried decided to take a step backwards and look at the droid that originally triggered the call. The robot in question did not have a face, just a screen. They implemented the style and developed a new bespoke body kit and "Clarkie" (Will's nickname) was born. They used a spot of breaking to prove Clarkie would be up to the task and sufficiently versatile for future development.

:Similar Difference

34 Pfingststaffel

Pfingststaffel

35 RBA

36 SKOLV

Soloth. Kantonaler
Orientierungslauf-Verband

Solothurner
Kantonaler
OL-Verband

---

34
:Client's Brief
Pfingststaffel wanted to give the brand more character.

:Design Philosophy
Custom designed typeface was used to reinforce the identity, two lines for better readability.

35
:Client's Brief
RBA wanted to restyle their corporate identity.

:Design Philosophy
Evolution, balance, consolidation, contemporary were the main aspects considered during the developing process.

36
:Client's Brief
SKOLV asked for redesigning the logotype based on the old logo.

:Design Philosophy
The logo was modernized, keeping its original character and symbolic quality.

:Similar Difference

37 Fases

38 CitID

39 ZARAGOZA Ayuntamiento

---

37
:Client's Brief
Fases sells furniture, especially dedicated to big offices or buildings. Futura must think in grown business men while making the proposal.

:Design Philosophy
MANIFIESTO FUTURA used geometrical forms that remind us some of the furniture that they sell. The icon was made to be used alone.

38
:Client's Brief
CitID's goal was to create a new unofficial rebranding for each city in the world, by a local artist. Big or small cities, known or unknown, all are equal. Calango was invited to represent Amsterdam, the capital of the Netherlands.

:Design Philosophy
The original logo of Amsterdam contains three "Saint Andrew's Crosses" meaning Valiant, Determent and Compassionate. Calango took that as a starting point and added different colored ribbons to represent the variety of cultures in Amsterdam who pursue those values together. Color inspiration came from the Dutch national flag.

39
:Client's Brief
Branding redesign to modernize the brand in the context of the Expo, optimize and standardize its use.

:Design Philosophy
Morillas updated the heraldry, emphasize Zaragoza, and established a universal language (City Council, Departments, Communication, Municipal Police).

:Similar Difference

## ⁴⁰ Star Plus

The Indian TV market is fiercely competitive, and as new channels started to win in the ratings, Star Plus asked venturethree to help them reinvent their brand, to reconnect with their core viewers: young women at the heart of the family.

From cold and corporate, to hot and aspirational, venturethree created a new identity for Star Plus, rooted in an optimistic, luxurious and emotional world, inspired by a ruby star.

The new identity freed the star from its containing device and positioned it centre-stage. The star itself lost its cold corporate appearance and took on that of a lush red jewel.

The new identity comes to life on-screen, as the ruby star glows, animates and turns to reveal strong female characters and dramas.

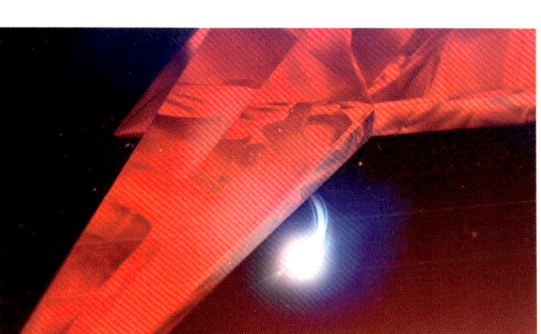

:Similar Difference

## [41] Sky

Eight years ago, Sky was doing some of the most exciting things in TV. But to look at their brand, you'd never know. The old brand portrayed Sky as a digital utility.

The focus was to launch a singular brand idea, big enough to excite customers year after year, and grow as Sky pushes the boundaries of TV, with innovation after innovation.

venturethree created a world-class brand, to help them bring the best entertainment, to the greatest number of people in the UK, Italy, Germany and Austria.

As part of Sky's evolution into an entertainment brand venturethree introduced the new glass mark, allowing Sky to bring its amazing content to life.

Over the years, venturethree has been working to establish Sky's leadership in entertainment, branding everything from the Sky masterbrand through to Sky+, Sky Broadband, Sky Talk, Sky Anytime, Sky+HD and now, 3D TV.

If you create a brand that's big and generous enough, there's no limit to where it can go. With the help of the new brand, Sky's customer base has gone up to 3 million subscribers in Germany, 5 million in Italy, and from 6 million to 10 million in the UK. That's one in three homes in Britain.

:Similar Difference

42 Linz

43 Exact

44 Transports Publics Genevois

42
:Client's Brief
Linz is an integral architecture firm dedicated to the architecture and management of private and public works.

:Design Philosophy
The goal was to design a dynamic, solid and "young" brand, connoting spatiality and projection.

43
:Client's Brief
Dutch business software company Exact wanted its logo (and entire visual identity) to express its overarching role in bringing back office and front office business process together to create value for its customers and their customers.

:Design Philosophy
The Exact logo conveys that bringing all aspects of a business process together creates value and underlines Exact's understanding of the SMB mentality, while the equal signs indicate the precision in everything they do.

44
:Client's Brief
The aim was to rejuvenate the image emitted by the previous visual identity in order to be more in tune with the reality of the company: TPG is a strong, dynamic, innovative and efficient company.

:Design Philosophy
To highlight the uniqueness of tpg, GVA Studio had a specific font created aspecialy for the company. Its symbol was created in a very specific logic that meets the following requirements: Sustainability, Identification, Accessibility.

:Similar Difference

45 Black Magic Sound

45
:Client's Brief
Black Magic Sound is a party concept concentrating in all styles of "black" music. Along with growth through the years came the need to develop a logo that could express this culture and concept efficiently to its broad audience and potential newcomers. The target audiences are anywhere between 17 and 30 with a wide knowledge of music culture.

:Design Philosophy
Modo's main focus when redesigning this logo was to try and honor or borrow inspiration from the classic and timeless labels of the 50-60-70's music industry: Motown, Blue Note, Fania, Island Records... throughout the process Modo agreed they would need a full logo with the whole three words (Black Magic Sound) and a second application with only the initials (BMS). They went through a wide range of options: from strictly geometrical to funky hand-drawn type. In the end they all agreed to a logo designed with the very much suitable font Lazybones. This font was created in 1972 by Letraset Studio and embodied everything the logo needed to reflect. The result was a very versatile logo that works amazingly in almost any color imaginable.

46 Boogie Nights

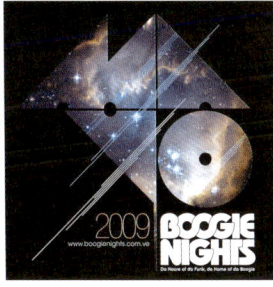
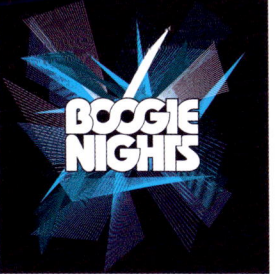

46
:Client's Brief
Boogie Nights wanted to update the logo without losing its original look and feel.

:Design Philosophy
Keeping the logo clean and simple enabled the logo to be easily used in various form.

:Similar Difference

47 Le Jardin Moderne

48 ZUMBI

49 VideoGamer.com

47
:Client's Brief
Le Jardin Moderne wanted to adapt the new logo with the new communication of the leaflet-poster.

:Design Philosophy
The logo was put in negative to highlight the light beams. The direction of the light beams was changed as well.

48
:Client's Brief
Zumbi is a freestyle martial arts movement, that needed a rebranding as they grew more professional. The brief was to create custom typography that represented the dynamic movements within martial arts, while still being solid.

:Design Philosophy
Calango took its inspiration from the Brazilian martial art, Capoeira,. Here the two fighters move so close together, their art becomes something between a dance and a well crafted clockwork.

49
:Client's Brief
The aim was to create an updated and spruced up version of the VideoGamer.com logo. The new logo should look modern but not very playful or too futuristic looking, and it must retain the four dots and the same color palette. It must be more original than just four dots.

:Design Philosophy
The brackets around the dots suggest a screen and the dots inside could be seen as gamers or a joy-pad. It could also be viewed as hands, a controller, a cross-hair, etc.

:Similar Difference

50 BIKOFE

50
:Client's Brief
The new owners of the BIKOFE bar wanted to refresh the image, but at the same time the new logo should not disrupt the continuity. More importantly the solution for the well-established social place needed to resonate well with the bar's image of the hippest place in town with a crowd of the super crytical young creative individuals.

:Design Philosophy
Before the redesign, the chameleon's characteristics were never really taken into account, but now Zek Crew have used these features as the starting point for the redesign. Just like the real chameleon, the logo can adapt to any surrounding just by placing the cut out image on almost any kind of surface. The chameleon's extended tongue was another feature of the real life animal that was put to use here. It can either be used as a logical continuation of the sign or just to border the logo's inscription.

:Similar Difference

## ⁵¹ HotFridge Records

**What does your client hope to achieve through redesigning the logo?**

The label was in the process of launching when they approached Superfried, so the time available for the development of their initial logo had been very short. They felt it was important to develop a strong brand identity as soon as possible before competing in the very tough and congested electronic music industry.

For us it was great to be involved from the very beginning since it is easier to maintain the purity and consistency of the ideas and desired look and feel. When a brand has been established for a long time there are often a lot of compromises to be made in the re-brand process which can be detrimental to quality of the final work.

**You added an icecream figure to the new logo. What do you think are the merits of applying pictogram in the logo?**

The pictogram can serve many purposes. At first it helps to commit a brand to memory since people generally remember images easier than words. Then, as the brand develops, it becomes possible to use the pictogram in isolation and render in different styles/mediums, whilst still maintaining recognition. This then lends itself to potential merchandise options. People are more likely to wear a tee with a cool icon/symbol rather than a blatant brand name in large letters.

**The colors of the previous logo are continued to use. Is it your client's requirement or the need of design?**

With regards to the colour scheme, for this brand we wanted it to feel bright, vibrant, free and less confined. This was necessary to reflect the eclectic nature of the label which is not restricted to one style or genre in their releases. Creating the logo with a multi-coloured gradient provided a wide colour range for selection. With this in place we were also able to adopt a changing colour scheme throughout the website, once again reflecting the high energy of the labels output.

**You've changed the typeface of the logo. What kind of new feeling do you think the new typeface try to approach?**

The typography is not actually based on a font, it was developed from scratch. Although more difficult, this method does ensure the logo is completely unique and enables us as the designers to maintain complete control. It was important that the typography felt friendly and open to all. It was also important that the lettering worked in unison with the icon to create the appearance of one harmonious logo rather than two separate entities forced together.

**How does the new logo respond to the brand's concept?**

We are really happy with the way this branding project has developed and feel the logo works well with the desired perception of the brand - but of course we would say that! Generally the feedback has been really positive and most importantly the client is happy!

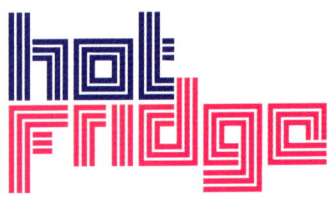

:Similar Difference

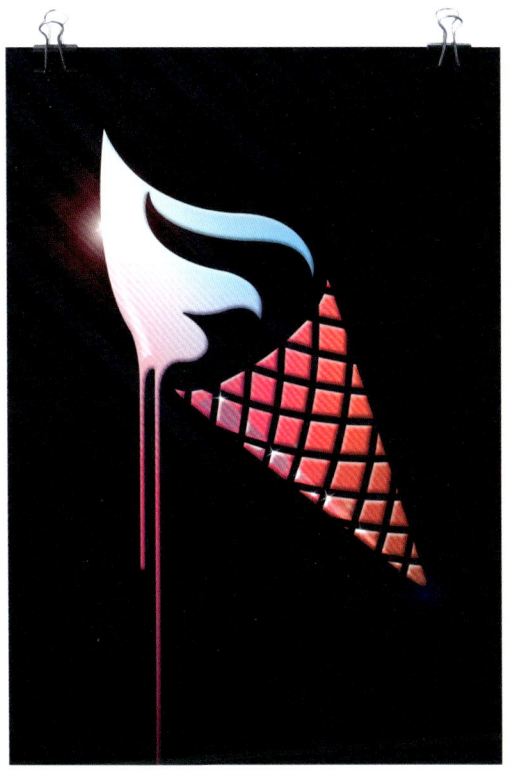

:Similar Difference

52 TMF Awards

52
:Client's Brief
The objective was to create a logo which is more generic and can be used for the next 5 years of TMF Awards.

:Design Philosophy
Keeping it simple and easy to adjust for future use while maintaining a distinct and fresh logo were the main things to be concerned with.

:Similar Difference

   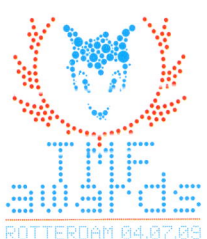

:Similar Difference

53 Hello Seahorse

54 Bombo

55 Rewind

53
:Client's Brief
The aim was to redesign for the "Lejos no tan lejos" album.
:Design Philosophy
A classic rock retro logo was developed.

54
:Client's Brief
Bombo wanted a logo with more impact, more strong and actual.
:Design Philosophy
To do the best with passion is Negro's design philosophy all the time.

55
:Client's Brief
The redesign was for a woman wearing Balenciaga leather pants and vintage Chanel bag in New York.
:Design Philosophy
The logo was created to be edgy and contemporary.

:Similar Difference

56 Metallica

57 Empik

**56**
**:Client's Brief**
Metallica wanted to return to their roots with their 2008 album Death Magnetic.

**:Design Philosophy**
Turner Duckworth returned to the original logo designed by band member, James Hetfield. They refined the letterforms, restored the iconic M and A and rotated the logo in space to make it more dynamic.

**57**
**:Client's Brief**
Empik decided to expand the chain stores offer, and thus, start working on the creation of new brand architecture and visual identification of individual subbrands. The aim was to transform point of sales into an icon and top of mind brand.

**:Design Philosophy**
The logo was created for brand icon. Individual typeface embodies the brand values. Comma-apostrophe in itself indicates a variety of services as opposed to previously functioning period involves the enumeration. The color kept to a minimum which makes the modified logo very visible against flashy ads. Clear, representative for the company.

:Similar Difference

58 Asian Clay Shooting Federation

59 Olympic Air

60 Le Musée Olympique

58
:Client's Brief
The ACSF wanted a brand identity that represents the vision, mission and values with which they serve their members. It must also be responsive to the changing needs of the modern association and encourage participation in the sport of clay shooting at all levels.

:Design Philosophy
The ACSF name has been uniquely rendered to incorporate a clay target and serves as the primary brand identity. To complement the text a new crest has been developed for the Federation. This crest derives its form from a first place ribbon and this brand mark serves as a universal symbol that signifies the goal of all athletes upon the quest to becoming an international champion.

59
:Client's Brief
Company took part in an international competition to re-brand the Greek national airline. The brief was to update Olympic Airline's identity while retaining the carrier's trademark multi-colored ring symbol.

:Design Philosophy
Company collaborated with font experts Dalton Maag to produce a bespoke font that maintains the essence of the existing logotype, but creates a more streamlined and sophisticated look. The overall visual language was designed to complement the current symbol and color scheme.

60
:Client's Brief
The aim was to create a visual identity and related guidelines for educational and promotional media destined to specific customers of The Olympic Museum. To establish a graphical cohesion of the identity through all media and improve the impact of The Olympic Museum on street media.

:Design Philosophy
GVA Studio concentrated on the logo and creation of a strong yet flexible structure around it. The aim was to focus one's attention on the Museum as a reliable, serious institution, aware of its history and looking to the future.

:Similar Difference

61 Prodigius Cinema

62 City of Randwick

 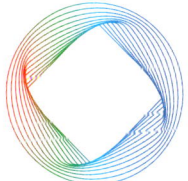

61
:Client's Brief
Prodigius Cinema is a film production company which combines talent and experience with young creativity. New logo must transmit the use of up to date technology and special component of magic.

:Design Philosophy
The brand had to be direct and clear, with simple elements that could generate shapes with more complexity.

62
Randwick is a city with a population of 130,000. Minale Tattersfield redesigned the logo of Randwick City Council and applied it into signage and entry markers for this city.

:Similar Difference

63 Yarra Trams

64 Global Canopy Programme

65 Smartree

63
Representing the Melbourne tram and leafy streets of Melbourne, Yarra Trams rebrand provides a new vitality to a moving Melbourne icon. Safety and sustainability formed a basis to a passenger focused brand language that strives to improve the passenger experience through clarity of messaging, tactical implementation and generosity of spirit.

64
:Client's Brief
Company have been working with the Global Canopy Programme for the last few years, developing their visual identity and a series of publications.

:Design Philosophy
Company designed the visual language to include various icons representing the characteristics and effectiveness of each proposal.

65
:Client's Brief
The growing, entrepreneurial, human resources company — at the time named generically humanresources.ro — was looking to get a differentiating name and graphic identity to suit its development plans.

:Design Philosophy
Smartree were also having a soft spot for the tree symbol, however still wanting to look cool and techno — the new name and the embedded T/tree marked on both counts. The identity became one of the most awarded and published Brandient logos.

:Similar Difference

66 Kreditbanken

 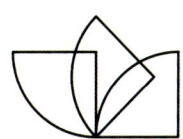

66
:Client's Brief
Kreditbanken, the local Danish bank needs new strong, recognizable identity to match the customer expectations of local, sustainable, conservative bank.

:Design Philosophy
Kreditbankens identity is based on its four values: flexibility, activity, proximity, independence.

:Similar Difference

## ⁶⁷ The Girl Scouts of the USA

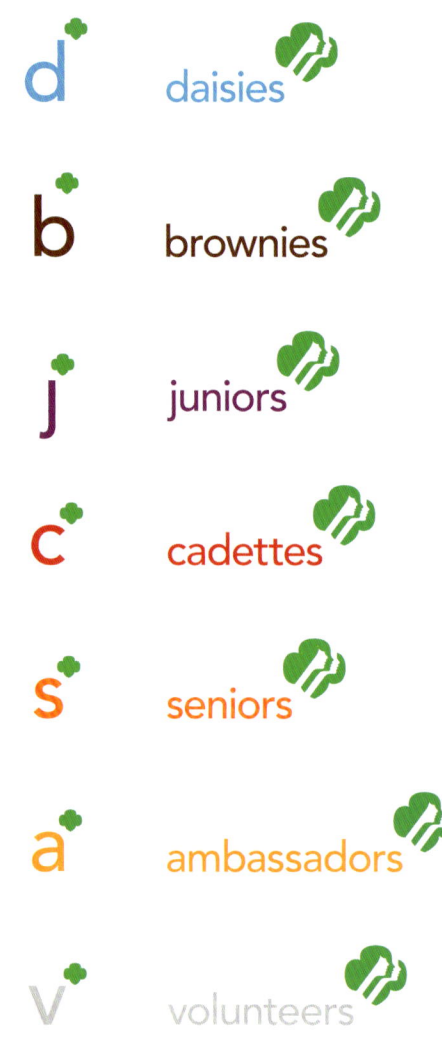

**There are only subtle differences between the new and the old logo. Is it due to the requirement from your client or the need of design?**

Established in 1912, the Girl Scouts of the USA is an iconic institution. Any work on the identity had to be sensitive to its rich history. Digging through the archive, we discovered that the trefoil has always played a key role in the brand identity. In 1978, legendary designer Saul Bass brilliantly redrew the trefoil. He softened the shape and transformed it into the now familiar positive-negative faces. Our challenge was to capitalize on the existing brand but make it relevant to a contemporary audience.

**Green is the main color of the logo. Who picked it? What is it for?**

The color green has been a part of Girl Scouts branding from the beginning. We amplified it by selecting a brighter, more vibrant shade, then simplified the core palette to green, white and black. Design is about discipline, for a new identity system to be effective, it had to live and die by just a few rules held closely.

**A series of logos of Girl Scout are also developed. But the characters are endowed with different colors. Are the colors chosen randomly or intentionally?**

The icon never changes color. It is always green. What does change color are the names of the grade levels. Girls graduate through different grade levels of Scouting, so we developed a brand system that syncs up with their existing programming language and helps differentiate a Brownie from a Junior.

**You also made the figure in the logo become the pattern of the whole identity. How did you come up with this idea?**

The goal of the new identity was to give them a complete and comprehensive brand language. Girls Scouts have long had a single beautiful mark, what we did was extend that mark into a complete system via the iconic trefoil shape. The trefoil is an ownable secondary design element that inspires limitless expression from patterns and textures to abstract compositions and meaningful visual metaphors.

**What do you and your client think of the end result?**

The new identity has given the whole organization a voice. The executives, the troops and the girls can all find their own, on-brand style within the system. We knew that if the brand properties could be unified, then the good works that Girls Scouts was doing would be better unified and the organization could have bigger impact. The public would take notice and the girls would be empowered.

:Similar Difference

:Similar Difference

girl scouts of historic georgia

girl scouts of the missouri heartland

girl scouts of nassau county

girl scouts of central and western massachusetts

girl scouts of north east ohio

girl scouts of california's central coast

girl scouts of the northwestern great lakes

girl scouts of minnesota and wisconsin river valleys

girl scouts of greater atlanta

girl scouts of black diamond

girl scouts of michigan shore to shore

girl scouts of eastern pennsylvania

girl scouts of greater chicago and northwest indiana

girl scouts of eastern oklahoma

girl scouts of north-central alabama

girl scouts of western ohio

girl scouts of northeastern new york

girl scouts of orange county

:Similar Difference

68 Hubrecht Institute

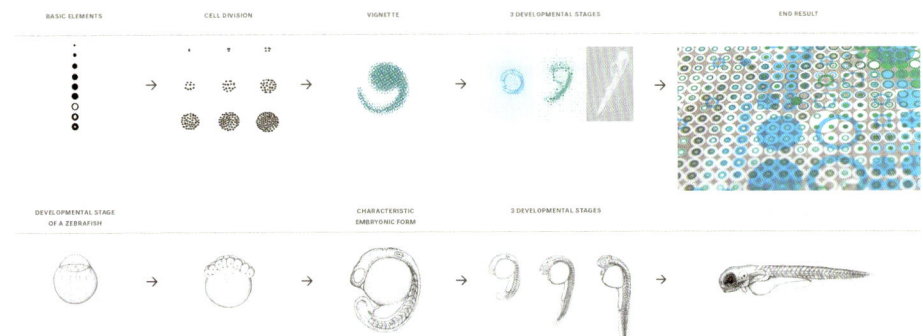

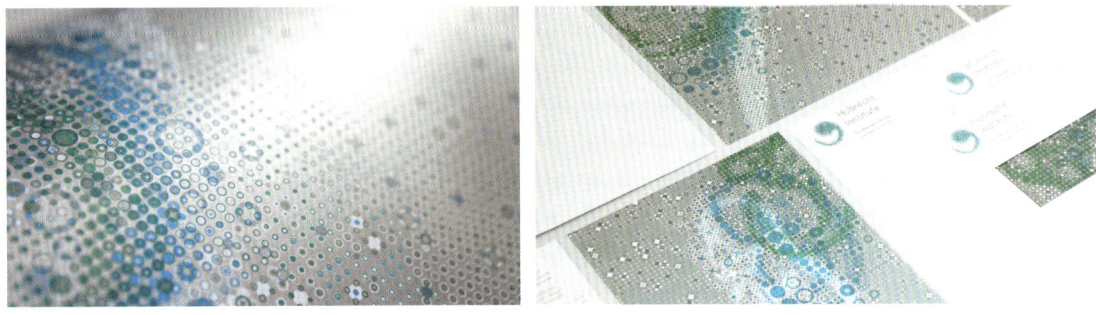

68
:Client's Brief
The aim was to develop a new visual identity for the Hubrecht Institute that reinforces the recognisability of the organization and adds to the global image as authority in the field of stemcell research and developmental biology. The deisgn should set an appropriate style and the modesty that fits within the scientific sector.

:Design Philosophy
The most elementary form from developmental biology was chosen as the foundation for the design of the new identity: the stem cell. Different circles represent the stem cells and are used as the "building blocks" for the new identity. In the logo they develop into an abstract form, which represents an embryo.

:Similar Difference

69 Firstunity

70 Illuminartis

71 Armani Exchange

69
:Client's Brief
As a boutique financial advisory firm, Firstunity provide bespoke wealth management services to individuals, families and firms. Their brief asked for a rebrand that illustrated the precision, excellence and sophistication of their services.

:Design Philosophy
Being subtle and refined, Firstunity's new identity system established the firm's impeccable standards. The precisely typeset wordmark, rich palette, delicate supporting pattern and use of letterpress on a decadent paper create a mature, meticulous collection.

70
:Client's Brief
Illuminartis wanted to combine the logotype with a new claim.

:Design Philosophy
Even in combination with the claim, the logo must keep its original simplicity and purism.

71
:Client's Brief
The fashion brand Armani Exchange had a problem: The letters A and X with a vertical slash between them, which had gained so much recognition over the years, had never been conceived as a logo. The letterforms were too light and disjointed to make an impact, especially when used with provocative photography.

:Design Philosophy
Chermayeff & Geismar reinvented the A|X mark, reversing it out of two boxes and giving it the strength to stand on its own. The redrawn letterforms are modern in their simplicity, with an elegant balance between thick and thin strokes. The result is a mark that reads as a visually powerful icon without any loss of brand equity.

:Similar Difference

72 HEP

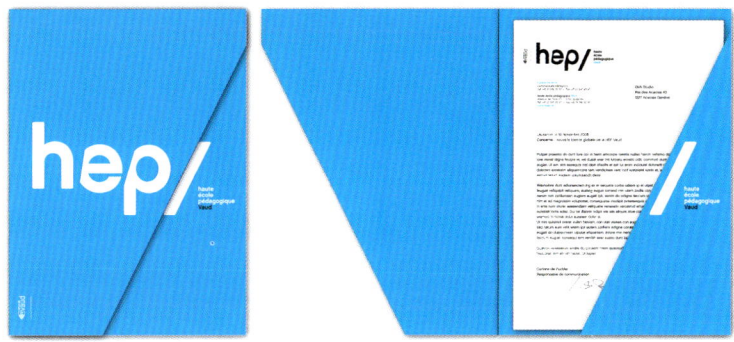

73 S4C

72
:Client's Brief
The Haute Ecole Pédagogique du Canton de Vaud wished to renew its logo and visual identity in order to federate the various internal emitters around one strong image that would convey the communicative personality of the school.

:Design Philosophy
The new logo was intended as an evolution of the previous one. Simple, round, more empathetic. GVA Studio integrated diagonals that converge into a focal point thus evoking the image of a fan. This image refers to the variety of opportunities offered by HEP Lausanne and was developed troughout the institution's communication mediums.

73
:Client's Brief
The objective was to rebrand the Welsh national TV channel and reconnect with its audiences in new ways.

:Design Philosophy
Proud Creative helped them to represent the Wales of today: vibrant, modern, progressive and bilingual.

:Similar Difference

74 Alg Börje

74
:Client's Brief
Swedish company Alg Börje, who specializes in skin care products that contains Icelandic algae, would like to have new fresh identity for their hydrating face cream.

:Design Philosophy
In our environmentally conscious society, skin care products of Alg Börje take a very good position with new identity that exudes its natural values, products purity and attracts discerning consumers, who care about wellness and healthy lifestyle.

:Similar Difference

75 Sanico

76 Corso 9

77 Biostase

75
:Client's Brief
Sanico required a new corporate image while maintaining the motif of the original logo of the business, a seahorse.

:Design Philosophy
The original logo of the business was a seahorse. Lavernia & Cienfuegos Design designed a new corporate image while maintaining this motif.

76
:Client's Brief
Corso 9 wanted to preserve the old label but with a refresh.

:Design Philosophy
R&MAG had redesigned the logo with a new geometrical grid.

77
:Client's Brief
Laboratoires Biostase, a French luxury cosmetics manufacturer, asked Inpublic to redesign its entire corporate identity in order to better support its relaunch as a business to consumer player.

:Design Philosophy
The final solution was designed using deconstruct methodology which is based on semiotics. Depending on their potential for generating brand equity, is a part of these elements was used into the new solution (e.g. color scheme) and reshaped the others (e.g. logotype, the orchid from the graphic symbol). The result is a visual identity reduced to the essence of the old one with a contemporary look and feel.

:Similar Difference

78 Centro Laser

79 The Irish Greyhound Board

80 Clear Channel

78
:Client's Brief
The company has changed marketing plan. So they needed new identity for marketing.

:Design Philosophy
R&MAG had designed a new logo but preserving the name.

79
:Client's Brief
Having inherited the regulatory Irish Greyhound Board logo, Creative Inc reorganised the brand structure and designed a new consumer identity which represents the entertainment aspect of the business without the need for type.

:Design Philosophy
Creative Inc used a silhouette of a greyhound with the industry coloured stripes contouring the body. A CGI greyhound was created to precisely follow the sinews and muscles of the animal. Hundreds of different variations of the dog were tested until they settled on the stance they felt appropriately conveyed the industry's central hero.

80
:Client's Brief
Clear Channel International is the world's largest out-of-home media company, with a presence in fifty countries. As a result, they needed an identity to bring a new coherence and consistency across all of their territories.

:Design Philosophy
The rebrand included an updated logo, with a redrawn symbol and wordmark, a contemporary sans serif font, a new vibrant colour palette; as well as a new illustration style, icons, bespoke photo library and brand guidelines.

:Similar Difference

81 Teethwhite

82 Montreux Cafe

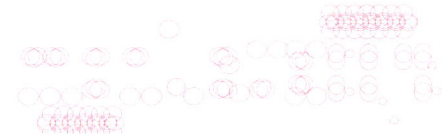

**81**
**:Client's Brief**
The aim was to rebrand the company to compete in a saturated market sector and to align the brand within the cosmetics industry.

**:Design Philosophy**
The initial design simplified the logotype, aligning it within the cosmetics sector. A selected colour palette and identity system was created to support the brand identity. The introduction of the hexagon was devised from the chemical symbol for teeth whitening ingredient. The colour palette allowed a flexible, yet consistent usage of the logotype.

**82**
**:Client's Brief**
Montreux Cafe had instructed BÜRO UFHO to redesign their existing identity which had legibility issues when applied small, keep existing elements like the wheat symbol, as well as to maintain the same number of seed heads in the existing logo.

**:Design Philosophy**
BÜRO UFHO felt the need to compact the logo as much as possible by varying the thickness of a similar condensed typeface to maximise legibility and help bridge the transition of the rebrand, as well as keeping elements like the wheat symbol that was used to subtly frame the wordmark.

:Similar Difference

83 EMUN

84 Design Ranch

85 Topagunea

83
EMUN is a language services company since 1997. di-da komunikakzioa (communication) helped them to restyle their logo.

84
:Client's Brief
Simply communicate the essence of a nationally recognized design and branding firm located in Kansas City, MO.

:Design Philosophy
Design Ranch uses the letter D and asterisk to suggest a cowboy's spur.

85
:Client's Brief
Brand redesign for Topagunea, a cultural organization that works to preserve and promote the Basque language.

:Design Philosophy
di-da komunikakzioa (communication) designed in fresh, colorful approach, showing diversity and originality.

## [86] Dahl Agenturer

Dahl Agenturer is a small family business that specializes in exclusive handpicked furniture and carpeting from many of Europe's finest designers.

They wished to keep the green colour from the existing logo, although it was adjusted somewhat at the end. They were also looking for something more sophisticated than the rather basic and generic logo they were already using in order to reflect the company better. After weeks of sketching the already established narrow rectangle from the old logo was chosen to use and replaced with the stem in the letter D.

To accompany the new logo a couple of different graphic patterns were introduced.

:Similar Difference

## [87] Holmegaard

Holmegaard is Denmark's most renowned producers of glassware. In 1825, Countess Henriette Danneskiold-Samsøe established Holmegaard with the philosophy that every Dane should have a beautiful drinking glass. Ever since then, Holmegaard has set design and industry standards. Today, as then, Holmegaard engages leading designers to create modern and functional glassware.

In 2008 Holmegaard was merged into Rosendahl Design Group. A group holding several reknown Danish design brands. This merger gave rise to a reestablishing and repositioning of the brand. First of all because the brand for the past 10 years has experienced declining sales and an aging brand perception, though nine out of ten Danes owns a Holmegaard product. Secondly because the Group already counted a glassware brand - Rosendahl - positioned to the more everyday consumer. The pivotal for the revitalising project became to ignite the spark within the DNA and positioning the brand as is and was - highend designed and functional mouthblown glassware for everyday usage.

This was the pivot point for the revitalizing project in order to assert the leadership position and revitalize its connection with the consumer - revitalizing it self product wise and in all its channels counting the brand's messaging, tone of voice, identity, imagery and tonality. Key questions was to redefine the answers to who are the highest priority targets? What is the single-minded promise and why should the target believe the new brand idea and appearance.

The client brief brought all elements influencing the brand perception into play. From pricing, standards of service, promotions, staff, advertising, packaging and of course the overall identity and branded elements. The task was to create the strategic platform and concept for the visual framework.

Make® supported Holmegaard in developing a new brand strategy defining a new value proposition. They created a brand platform - "celebrating the legacy" - without letting the past define the brand. The pivot point was taken from brand surveys and internal interviews. It was clear that the brand should target a younger audience. A new strategy was needed to project the strong, emotional quality and Nordic design values present in the products. Therefore, the key objective was to transform an old fashioned brand and to grasp the sparkle in the products. To turn an occasional usage of the products to an everyday experience without losing the high-end design and quality feeling.

Holmegaard's communication platform is the brand itself. A transparent and glasslike look with a feminine feel. As the color red historically was a dominant part of the universe this was converted to a thin red line reflecting the legacy. The transparent and golden scheme enhances the reworked logo and all these elements portray Holmegaard as an authentic, fresh and personal brand. The photography is a striking feature; capturing moments of use.

The identity is implemented on all branded elements and the brand identity also set the tone when one of the blockbuster products - Future Glass - was brought to life in a 29 second film. Again simplicity, usage and common situations was the focal point in order to let the core strategy and identity deliver the brand's special qualities appropriately translated to the screen - package, wrapping paper, leaflets or whatever material needed.

As all material is kept tight and still conducted by Make® in close collaboration with Holmegaard they can continue to reinforce and develop the identity. The strong visual concept enables the brand to have longevity both as a broadcast advertisement and as versatile and engaging brand content across media.

:Similar Difference

 NO.5 MINIMA COCOON

:Similar Difference

88 Herradura

89 Monterossa

90 Distillerie Franciacorta

88
One of Mexico's oldest and most respected tequila brands — Herradura sought to better reflect the super-premium quality of its beverages. This brand revitalization strives to present the rich legacy of a 140-year-old brand, to a 21st century world. In a successful client and agency partnership, Duffy & Partners focused design efforts on evolving packaging, while the client team created broader marketing and promotional materials.

89
:Client's Brief
Monterossa is a Franciacorta cellars.

:Design Philosophy
Raineri Design has completely redesigned the brand of Monterossa, harmonizing curves, sign cleaning and enriching the graphic layout. Raineri started with a design path redesigning and repositioning of the brand.

90
Distillerie Franciacorta is a Historic Italian Wine Distillery since 1801. Raineri Design helped them to restyle their logo and the corporate image.

:Similar Difference

91 Melazic

91
:Client's Brief
The objective was to position the brand Melazic to its target.

:Design Philosophy
After months of cogitation, exchanges, brainstorming, discussion, the United Melazic inaugurates its new identity and the full range that goes with it! Tomography, logo, stationery, stickers, and so on, the brand values are now displayed on all communication for the United pleasure of Melanie and Princesses Soizic Romero, founders and directors of the brand.

:Similar Difference

92 Huttons

:Client's Brief
Huttons is a retail chain with a varied product range from scented candles and women's clothes to high-end furniture.

:Design Philosophy
The rebrand was a challenging brief since despite 80% of customers being female it was important not to alienate men. Superfried achieved this balance with effective use of colour and subtle iconography.

:Similar Difference

93 UK Skills

94 Armada

95 Brosway

93
:Client's Brief
Through competitions and awards, UK Skills champion the exceptional talents of the nations skilled individuals. To align itself appropriately with the events it delivers, UK Skills required a new identity.

:Design Philosophy
As the engine behind all of the events, the UK Skills identity is rarely seen alone, it therefore requires distinction and authority, as well as simply communicating the objective of all its competitions; to recognise and award excellence.

94
:Client's Brief
Armada wanted a logo which is of uniformity and timelessness.

:Design Philosophy
Saša Stucin made the logo raw and stable.

95
:Client's Brief
Brosway, an Italian manufacturer of jewels and watches, after seven years needed a radical redesign of the original logo, that mixed in inappropriate way the first word in Bauhaus style letterforms and the second with a calligraphic pen stroke.

:Design Philosophy
A single customized typeface, based on the Helvetica Extended's proportions, was used to simplify the shape, trying to maintain some details that remembers the original logo.

:Similar Difference

## [96] Murmure

# MURMURE

# MURMURE

*communication, design & art*

**Many designers find it hard to design for themselves. Did you come across any difficulty when redesigning your logo?**

Of course it was hard at the beginning. We wanted to say so much and the logo had to be so simple and easy to remember. We tried to express in many ways our apt for refined design, our persuit of innovation and our love for typography.

A logotype based on a very fancy and contemporary font was the most potent choice. It combined the elegance and the strength of a letterpress used for titles and text with the simplicity of our name.

**You've changed the typeface of the logo. What kind of new feeling do you think the new typeface try to approach?**

The new typeface is a bit stronger than the old one, and serif is also underlined in order to put it up. Thereby, it becomes more a logo font than a title font.

**The new logo has inherited the colors of the old one (black and white). Why did you continue to use these colors?**

We chose to keep black and white as the main colors because they express both sobriety and elegance.

**The "Murmure" logo can be classified as glyph logo since there's no specific figure in it. What do you think the merit of this kind of logo?**

Glyph logos are very simple and efficient. Their main quality is to highlight the company's name which in our case says also a lot of our interest in Street Art and the poetic side of some of our works (mur means wall in French and murmure is a whisper). Traits completes the picture.

**In the application of the new logo, "M" seems to be the variation of the new logo, and is used even more than it. Why is that?**

M is obviously the initial of Murmure. It is also simpler to recognize and it serves as a mark, a token, a cachet. It sometimes allows us to play with textures, media and editing process within the surface of the letter like in the puch hole greeting cards we made to celebrate year 2011.

:Similar Difference

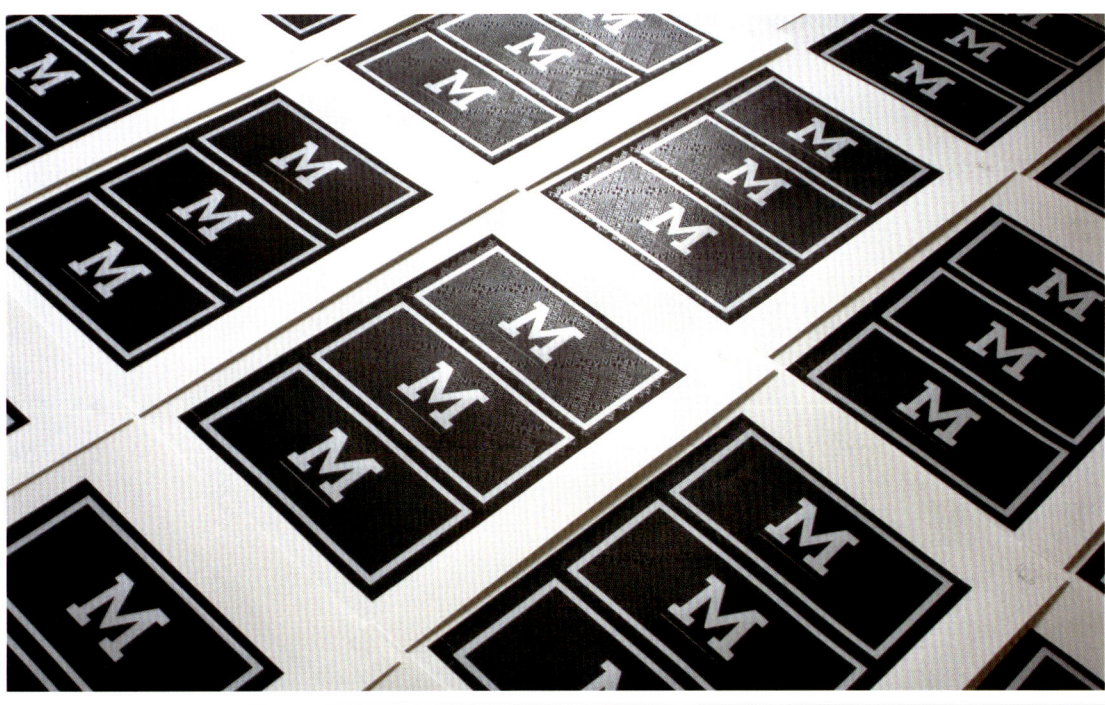

:Similar Difference

97 Libreria Formatos Bookstore

# liiibreríiiaformatos

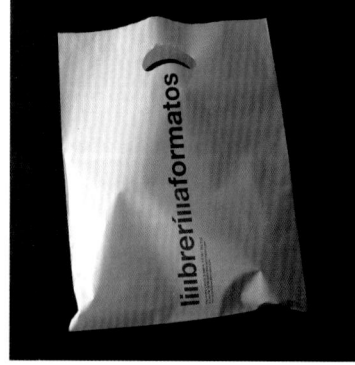

97
:Client's Brief
Libreria Formatos Bookstore specialized in books for design, architecture and photography.

:Design Philosophy
The objective was to design a simple marking easily applied to different media, which in turn graphically summarized the product the company sells. I worked the concept of books on a shelf repeating the "i" and simulating the books on a shelf.

:Similar Difference

98 Canvas Group

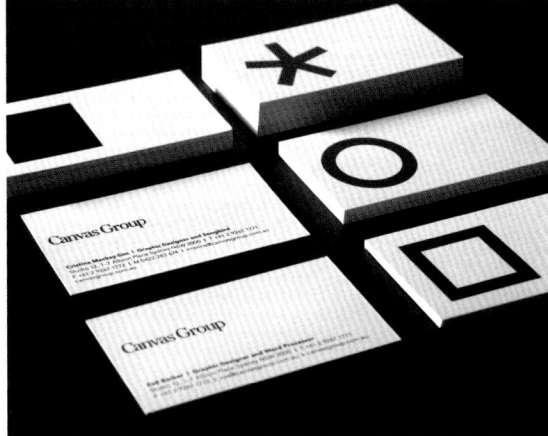

99 The Viral Company

TVC

---

**98**
**:Client's Brief**
A self-imposed brief to reinvigorate the Canvas Group brand, with an emphasis on the "Group", absent in the old wordmark.

**:Design Philosophy**
Balancing elegant typography, a stark palette and lashings of personality was key to this rebrand; the latter point achieved through the playful language that is now a key component in Canvas Group communications.

**99**
**:Client's Brief**
The Viral Company wanted a logo that was combining the letters T+V+C in a stylish but yet playful way.

**:Design Philosophy**
This is an emblem – making a bold confident impression, as the same time as sending the thoughts to how fashion brands often combine letters into shapes.

:Similar Difference

100 EFFP

101 OSBORNE

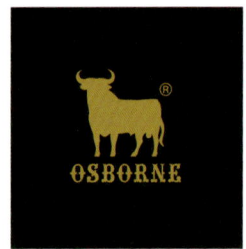

102 PronoKal

100
:Client's Brief
EFFP provides consultancy to the agricultural and food industry. They strive to build bonds between these two industries, to make both more efficient. EFFP needed help to differentiate themselves from other consultants in the sector.
:Design Philosophy
The resulting black and white identity is bold, pioneering, confident and revolutionary, all attributes EFFP aspire to.

101
:Client's Brief
The aim was to define the new brand of a group that's anchored in historical activities.
:Design Philosophy
Character, bull, tradition, current, quality were the key words involved in the redesign.

102
:Client's Brief
The aim was to redefine the brand design and packaging, and change the perception and communication line, with new presentation of the pack showing the values of PronoKal.
:Design Philosophy
Quality, serious, medical, healthy, tasty were the key words involved in the redesign.

:Similar Difference

103 AÏZONE

AÏZONE
AÏZONE
AÏZONE

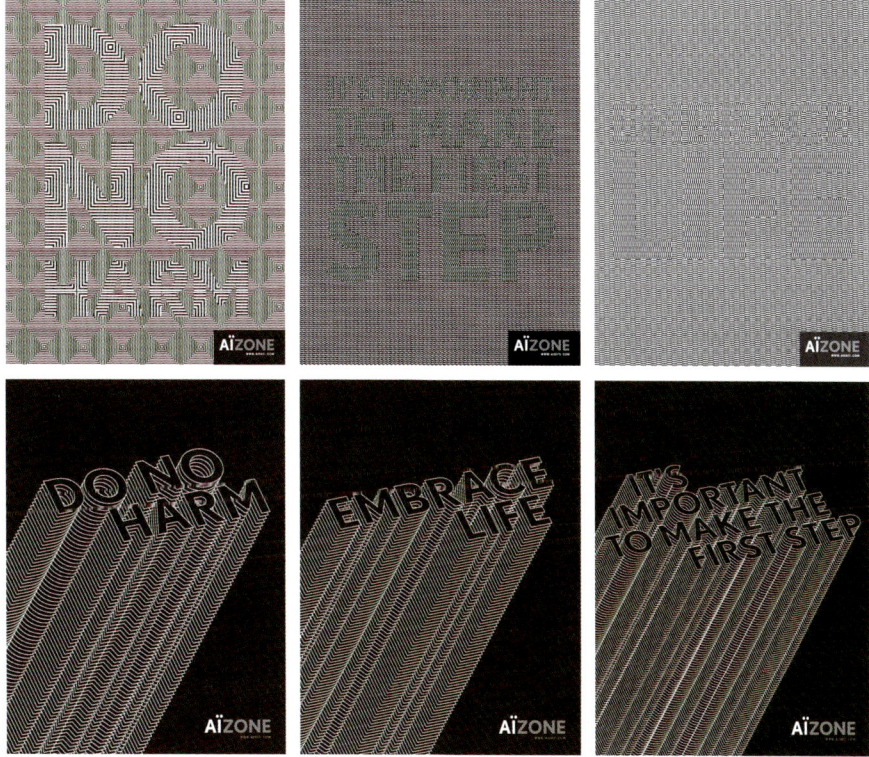

103
The AÏSHTI brand which includes AÏZONE, and AÏSHTI Mini, was looking to raise the abr of their visual identity. In order to improve upon their product, which is considered as symbol of luxury in the Middle East. Brand identity for AÏSHTI, a Beirut-based luxury retailer with store locations throughout the Middle East. This identity includes the parent AÏSHTI brand, as well as its young adult brand AÏZONE and its children's brand AISHTI Minis.

:Similar Difference

## [104] Memoma

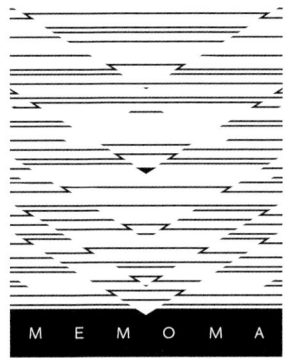

:Similar Difference

Since the beginning of the project, Memoma was the design studio as well as the client. So Memoma had a customer-supplier relationship. This relationship led to high demands and different needs of other projects they have done. Their goal was to create a completely innovative visual identity that was totally different from previous identity. A simple, authentic, elegant and almost corporative identity that required the minimum of materials for production. Memoma were also looking for a strong identity that supports, speaks and exalts itself both in digital and print media, while reflecting the personality of their work.

If every sound or image carries a wrap of known and used feelings and that predispose the recipient to boredom despite the best efforts of every innovation, a break in the restricted circle of pure images managed to conquer the infinite variety of creation.

Under this parameter, Memoma worked out a way to synthesize ideas and ideals that represent them as a studio, such as "Noise", "TV Interference", "Breakdown", "Fracture", "Honesty", "Dynamic" and at the same time to rescue some elements of previous logo, in this case the diagonals of the letter "M", forms three-sixths of their name. Within the process and as a final goal, Memoma wanted a (really) different, solid and timeless logo that breaks with established rules of their environment, using only two colors and pure substrates for stationery. At the end they still think that all the above concepts are what they are.

:Similar Difference

105 Fox Johnston

FOX JOHNSTON    Fox Johnston

105
:Client's Brief
Fox Johnston push the boundaries of contemporary architecture, approaching every project as an opportunity to further their discipline. Their new identity needed to support this ambition and drive.

:Design Philosophy
Sophisticated, yet straight-up, the new identity is clean and contemporary. Its bold serifs and heavy stroke weight make it approachable and unpretentious. A vibrant colour palette establishes Fox Johnston as an innovator, while the embossed business card translates architecture to paper.

:Similar Difference

106 NightHawk

107 Mannheimer Swartling

108 Samuels Yoelin Kantor

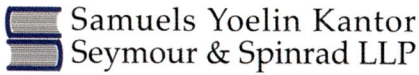

106
:Client's Brief
Serving roughly 26% of the hospitals in the United States, NightHawk looked to validate its rapid growth with a renewed excitement surrounding the brand image.

:Design Philosophy
The modern wings evoke both expediency and protection, while the "evening" color palette further reinforces the name and supports the necessary trust and reliability for this national, medical technology brand.

107
:Client's Brief
Mannheimer Swartling wanted their visual identity to communicate their values based on world-class quality, long-term business focus and a team spirit in which cooperation takes place in a down-to-earth manner and across boundaries, and where there is respect for one another's expertise, priorities and personalities.

:Design Philosophy
Dolhem Design took advantage of the existing environment of tradition and knowledge. To ensure that the profile instilled an up-to-date feeling, they created a modern symbol.

108
:Client's Brief
With a name change, Jeff Fisher LogoMotives originally created a new logo for this law firm in 1997. Another name change, a move to a new office space, in 2011 required an update of the logo design and change to the name Samuels Yoelin Kantor, LLP.

:Design Philosophy
Retaining the "S" icon, representing the Samuels name and two law books, for a historical perspective; the redesign of the logo required introducing more contemporary type treatments and colors.

:Similar Difference

109 Mobil Oil Corporation

110 Amazon.com

111 St George International

109
For Mobil, the evolution to a clean, modern graphic look and contemporary architecture emerged from a distinct change in personality and a desire to be welcomed in post-war suburban developments.

The new Mobil signature, with its distinct red "O", was made a universal symbol everywhere the Mobil name appeared, from service stations to packages to office stationery.

The program was built around the logo, a specially designed alphabet, a clear policy for color, and a comprehensive design approach that integrated new graphics with new architecture.

110
:Client's Brief
At a time when Amazon.com had just started to expand beyond bookselling, they wanted a new logo that signified two things: 1) Amazon.com's first priority is customer service, and 2) The company sells much more than books.

:Design Philosophy
Turner Duckworth infused personality into the logo by turning the "frown" of the downward underline upside down – literally making the logo smile. This conveyed "customer service", while also linking the "a" and the "z", communicating "everything from A to Z". They created an entire hand drawn alphabet so that Amazon.com could create logos for each country.

111
:Client's Brief
Long-standing London language school St George International (SGI) needed to update its identity, and create a brand that could support national and international expansion.

:Design Philosophy
To emphasise the importance of SGI's London location Mammal combined images of the city with speech bubbles and by photographing students with the speech bubbles near London landmarks, they created an identity that could feature different audiences and messages. The palette of red, white and grey reflects classic London colours.

:Similar Difference

112 bpost

113 ART-CAPITAL

114 Delta

112
:Client's Brief
De Post-La Poste sought to develop a new name, brand strategy, and visual and verbal identity that would unlock the value behind the business strategy and signal to the world that the business was ready to compete after full market liberalization.

:Design Philosophy
A new name was created: bpost will replace De Post-La Poste as of June 17th, 2010. In addition renaming the company, the visual and verbal identity, including logo, has been modernized to represent a dynamic company in a complex and modern digital world.

113
:Client's Brief
The key challenge was rebranding ART-CAPITAL.

:Design Philosophy
The brand platform is growing and moving to the aim pointer — a symbol of developed button symbolizes push and movement. The XCLV brand formula is: Logo is a button of growing and moving to the aim, to next level. Red color is dominant.

114
:Client's Brief
The main objective of the project was to coincide with the airline's emergence from a Chapter 11 restructuring, Delta wanted a strategic reposition, image revitalization and customer experience redesign.

:Design Philosophy
The new logo was designed to convey a renewed strength and confidence and modernization of the airline to both customers and its employees. The simplified all-red symbol and all-uppercase logotype visually reinforce a more sophisticated, directed and globally appropriate expression while being considerate of the airlines extensive heritage. The Delta symbol is further leveraged through a dynamic cropped livery treatment that speaks to momentum, growth and optimism.

:Similar Difference

115 Time Warner Cable

116 Intrum Justitia

117 Crèdit Andorrà

---

115
:Client's Brief
The Brand Union, working with Time Warner Cable's marketing team to gain a deep understanding of the mission that drove their practices, created a refreshed visual identity system that activated that mission both internally and externally by highlighting the vibrant and young-minded tone of the brand.

:Design Philosophy
The Brand Union shed the category's complex conventions by refreshing the eye and ear symbol and developing a vibrant color palette, a proprietary typeface, and a unique photographic style to reflect the simplicity that technology should bring to the everyday lives of consumers.

116
:Client's Brief
The assignment was to unify the organization, 24 countries, under one brand with a common logotype. The new visual profile should communicate the basis of Intrum Justitia's strategic plan and values - fair, customer-oriented, target-oriented, ambition and know-how.

:Design Philosophy
Intrum is symbolized by what looks like a welcoming person with open arms. The lines of previous logotype symbolized longitude and latitude. The lines were modified to form the letter "j" for Justitia. The globe stands for Intrum Justitia's international operations and the company's overall view. The green and warm colours stand for growth.

117
:Client's Brief
Crèdit Andorrà wanted to modernize the brand personality to consolidate leadership. Capturing the young segment.

:Design Philosophy
Soundness, tradition, contemporariness and country were the key words involved in the redesign.

118 Voices of Youth

# Voices of Youth

 Child Rights
 Gender Equality
 Violence

 Millennium Development Goal
 Disabilities
 Water, Environment & Sanitation

 Education
 Indigenous People's Rights
 Unite for Climate

 HIV and AIDS
 Commercial Sexual Exploitation

119 Glaad

---

118
:Client's Brief
UNICEF's Voices of Youth program strives to offer all children and adolescents a safe space where their voices will be heard: a place online where they can explore, learn, discuss, and grow together.

:Design Philosophy
Hyperakt created a comprehensive branding platform for Voices of Youth, including a logo and a system of symbols and color schemes that represent the various issues the Voices of Youth dialogue will revolve around.

119
:Client's Brief
Glaad needed a simple, clear way to identify the organization as the media arm of the movement, build awareness for their media expertise and recognition for the range of activities and programs they sponsor.

:Design Philosophy
The new identity symbolizes how the organization amplifies the voice of the community, playing off a recognized symbol for communication. The logo suggests movement, growth and momentum – all key ingredients in the fight for equality and representation. The four color versions of the logo represent the diversity, energy and passion of the community.

:Similar Difference

## [120] Lawson-Fenning

Lawson-Fenning — brand identity system through marketing collateral and campaigns. Lawson-Fenning is a Los Angeles based furniture and furnishings company with strong vintage influences. The company's rich aesthetic of modern shapes combined with classic traditional details captures the eclectic and often contradictory aspects from the Los Angeles area. The shop's line of furniture and accessories borrow the glam of old Hollywood, the playful forms and materials of mid-century modernism and the visual efficiency of Stark Modernism. The Lawson-Fenning team are also collectors of a well curated selection of vintage furniture and accessories from the 40's, 50's and 60's.

TomTor Studio's design process began with concept work sessions and interviews with the client at Lawson-Fenning. The client was very clear regarding the need to build their business of upholstered furniture and accessories and design the lines within the company's brand. The influence of the identity and marketing needed to incorporate vintage and resonate within the periods of the 40's, 50's and 60's. TomTor Studio developed a brand language that had influences from those periods by first exploring and developing the concept ideas of the mark. The mark created needed to have a unique look and communication about the brand. TomTor Studio landed on creating a mark that resembled a simplified holly flower. It was important that the holly flower was simplified in a line of seven with a Stark Modernism feel to it. The type for the identity was wanted to have a strong vintage feel but still communicate playfulness and mid-century modernism.

:Similar Difference

121 Cehba

121
:Client's Brief
Cehba is a clinic with a modern line, and soft.

:Design Philosophy
To do the best with passion is Negro's design philosophy all the time.

122 Sanipur

123 Dublin City Council

124 Egalsa

122
Sanipur is a water treatment company. Raineri Design helped them to restyle their logo and the corporate image.

123
:Client's Brief
Following a legislative requirement to change the former name of Dublin Corporation to Dublin City Council, Creatine Inc were employed to create a new, more contemporary identity which could be applied across the Council's wide and varied range of activities and publications.

:Design Philosophy
Creatiue Inc tried to keep it simple to allow for a very elaborate identity programme.

124
:Client's Brief
The aim was to redesign the logo of Egalsa creating an evolution of existing logo.

:Design Philosophy
Unlimited Creative Group created a logo that represents the philosophy and what the company sells: packaging solutions.

:Similar Difference

125 Domo

125
:Client's Brief
Domo commissioned Brandient to create a new visual identity and to lead the rebranding process that marked the company's transition from entrepreneurship to corporation.

:Design Philosophy
The new identity of the leading retailer — remarkably the two striped balls in the logo — infused the brand with a playful and friendly personality. Retail graphics were developed as a meta-language to enhance brand's recognition and favorability.

:Similar Difference

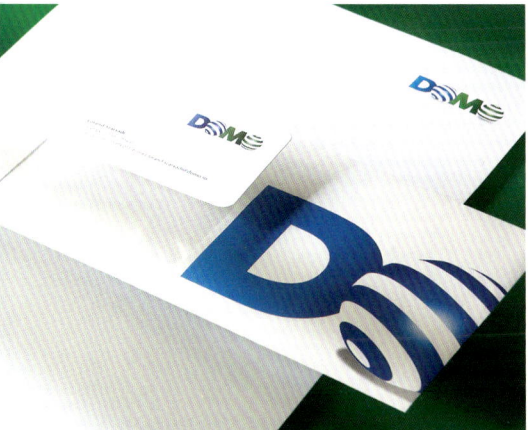

:Similar Difference

126 VYP

126
:Client's Brief
VYP is a consulting company specialized in the petroleum business.

:Design Philosophy
NNSS worked on a sober but elegant brand. The bar makes reference to the different ground layers. Design proposal based on a strong company concept.

## [127] Monarch Airlines

**What is the client's requirement on redesigning the logo?**

It should reflect to modern attitude of a low-cost airline with the long lasting heritage of one of the oldest airlines in Great Britain. Straight forward, no cheat, no hidden agenda brand.

**You applied purple and yellow as the theme color of the identity. It looks so bright and young and different from the other identities of airline companies. Could you please explain the reason why you use them as the theme color?**

Entering and re-establishing Monarch in the low-cost marketplace as an airline with no hidden agenda, and for the rebrand to stand out, we decided very early on to leverage the existing colour palette, but making it fresher, more vibrant (like the attitude the Monarch employees have) and warmer. This allows us to immediately standout in the marketplace (eg. airport with a multitude of other airline logos), have a big visual impact in a crowded environment (newspapers with lots of ads, airports with lots of signs and advertising all over), and foremost own a colour palette that can't be used by any competitor.

**Did you encounter any challenge when designing the new logo?**

Modernising an existing logo is never an easy task. Too much is at stake, and many people (employees, stakeholders) have been living with their logo for a long time. In our case it wasn't much of an issue, since the whole new positioning and the rebrand called for a modernisation. Simplifying the use of the logo as well as how many individual assets need to be aligned with it, makes it much more successful. And having a great client that supports all our ideas and thinking was great!

:Similar Difference

128 Blow

128
The aim was to completely redesign the brand, including identity, architecture and packaging to help define this new category and defend Blow's position as the original New York blow dry bar. The challenge was to blend high-frequecy, low cost and luxury.

:Similar Difference

:Similar Difference

:Similar Difference

:Similar Difference

## ¹²⁹ Mercato Antiques

Owner, Mary Lies fills her shop with directly imported high-end Italian antiques radiating with history, culture and class. To communicate the essence of her store, Design Ranch chose the name Mercato (market) and paired it with a beautifully comprehensive brand. They built in layers of artwork, photography and handmade detail—rooted in found treasures embodying the rich experience of antiquing. Now, Mercato's customers walk into the shop and fully experience Italian luxury, sans jet lag.

:Similar Difference

130 Thymes

131 The Cradle

132 Launch Collective

### 130
**:Client's Brief**

After two decades of success, Thymes needed to reinvent itself to maintain leadership in a cluttered category. Design efforts began with positioning and brand identity work and extended through marketing materials and across a product line of over 20 collections.

**:Design Philosophy**

A new look, coupled with fresh products and new ideas spurred renew interest in this brand and its desire to show a true sense of caring about the art of living a beautiful life.

### 131

The visual language from brandmark to photographic style, from design layout and grids to production techniques is informed by the brand identities of 5 star hotels and health spas. These rich visual cues are aimed at connecting with the premium "parents-to-be" market who wished to have access to the highest possible standard of clinical care and be pampered and spoilt during birth recovery, and were happy and willing to pay for that. The brand voice needed to signal something new and different to the market, but at the same time create immediate trust and belief, with a nuturing personal feel. The new identity was implemented across stationery, signage, brochure and website.

### 132
**:Client's Brief**

Launch Collective wanted a fresh yet sophisticated brand identity that would appeal to their client base: the fashion industry but also show that they are business savvy consultants.

**:Design Philosophy**

The design of the logo was inspired by the word "launch". The elongated type was created to give the impression of upward movement and to conjure an impression of haute or elegance.

:Similar Difference

133 Parad

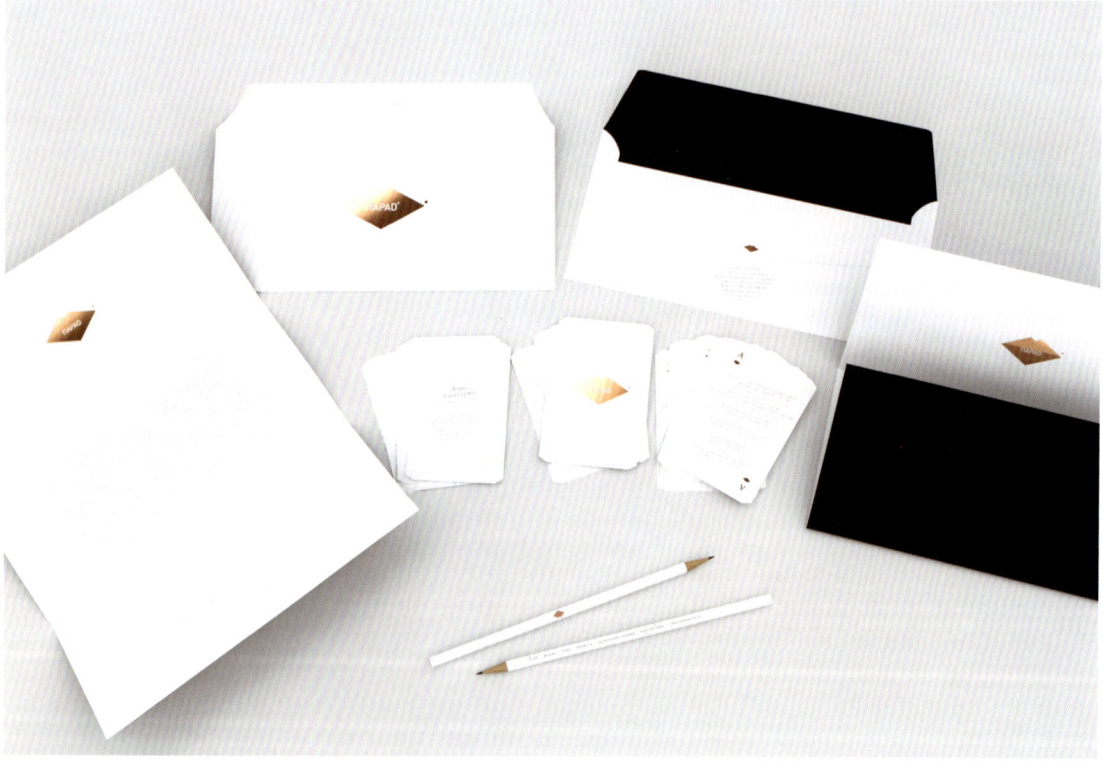

133
:Client's Brief
"Parad" is a network of fashion boutiques with a friendly face. It is focusing on women shoes. They were willing to boost visual communication even more and make the brand a bit more glamorous.

:Design Philosophy
This logo is a part of rebranding Proekt's performed for "Parad" boutiques. The rebranding touched all elements of "Parad" image: corporate ID (logo, business cards, discount cards, shopping bags, price tags, letterheads, envelopes, hat boxes, pencils and notepads), boutique interiors and website. The logo represents stylized female lips with a beauty spot — a graphic quintessence of femininity and mystique.

134 Pitcher & Piano

# PITCHER & PIANO

# PITCHER
# &
# PIANO

135 JEAN BOURGET

---

**134**
**:Client's Brief**
Pitcher & Piano wanted a new logo to capture a quintessentially British mood for a chain of premium pubs.

**:Design Philosophy**
The existing logo was very restrictive because of its size and proportions, so Studio Output tightened it up, stacked it to make a stronger unit, increased the weight and crafted some of the characters.

**135**
**:Client's Brief**
JEAN BOURGET is a designer who designs children's clothing from France. Its collections deviate noble materials, crafting original combinations to create everyday luxury for children. A unique know-how that its old logotype did not convey at all.

**:Design Philosophy**
In order to bring back genuine French elegance and childhood spirit at the core of the brand, BAYADERES created a new script and a new brand icon, the childish hand drawing star, as a universal symbol of dreams & poetry. The color palette has also been lightly soften.

:Similar Difference

136 CHEUNG NING

137 RPW Law

138 Where They At

136
:Client's Brief
CHEUNG NING, an international diamond processing company, finished transforming from a traditional family business to an international listed enterprise. So they needed to upgrade and optimize their identity to become more international.

:Design Philosophy
CN is the abbreviation of CHEUNG NING. The typeface absorbed and inherited the "dragon" element of the previous logo. The "dragon" element got simplified and blended with the typeface.

137
:Client's Brief
RPW wanted an updated, fresh look.

:Design Philosophy
When redesigning the logo, Garrett Patz thought that law always came full circle.

138
:Client's Brief
The aim was to bring a less femine style to this New Orleans Hip-Hop documentary photography exhibition.

:Design Philosophy
Erik Kiesewetter wanted to call back to the style of the 1990's hip-hop record label companies of the South.

:Similar Difference

139 National Maritime Museum

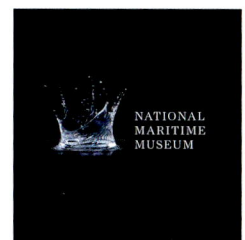

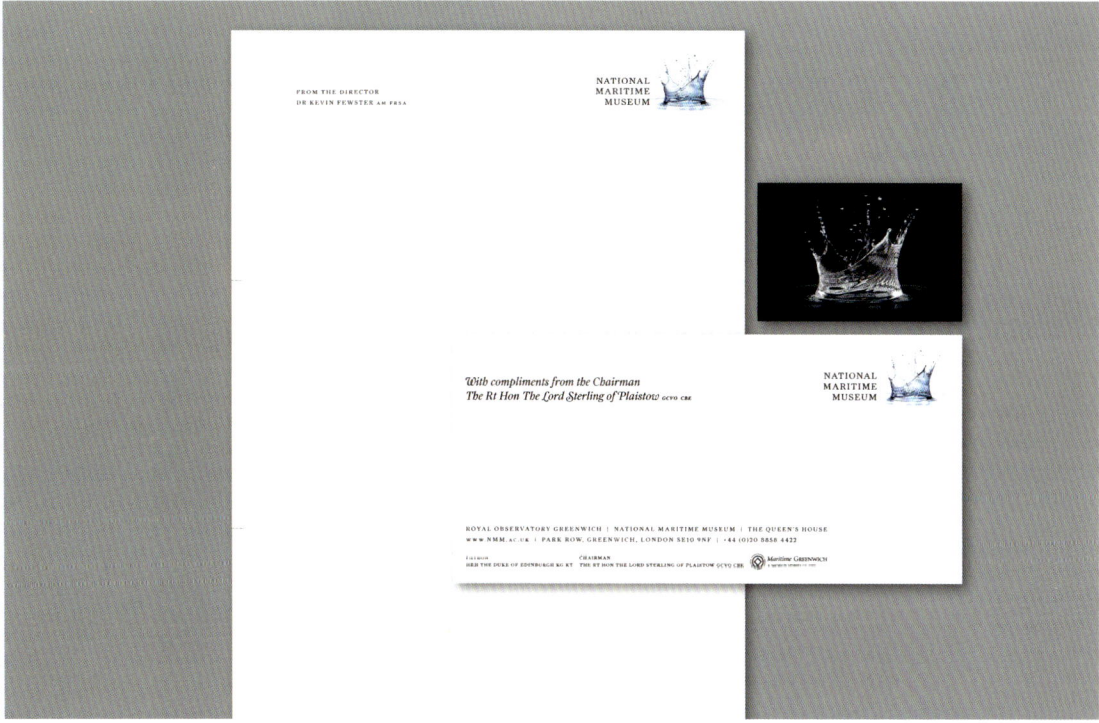

139
:Client's Brief
SomeOne was appointed as brand strategist and identity consultant following a four-way pitch in April 2010 to rebrand and rename The National Maritime Museum, which is one of the largest museums in the world on this theme and one of the most popular attractions in the UK, along with rebranding The Royal Observatory, Peter Harrison Planetarium and The Queen's House.

:Design Philosophy
The identity uses a splash image to reflect the global reach of discoveries about navigation, timekeeping, astronomy and technology made in Greenwich. The splash has different colour variations to denote the Museum's different sites, using sea-blue for the Maritime Museum, gold for the Queen's House and Royal purple for the Royal Observatory.

:Similar Difference

140 Id doma

id:doma

**id:**doma

**:d**bcčoefghijklmnaprsštu

**:a**bcčdefghijklmnoprsštu

**id:**d　　　o　　　　m　　a

140
:Client's Brief
Id doma asked for a timeless, conceptual, evolving and airy logo.

:Design Philosophy
The new logo is discreet and timeless. Each letter within the logotype carries its own message, which the company tries to send directly (d for doma as home, o for oblikovanje as design, m for magazin as magazine and a for arhitektura as architecture).

:Similar Difference

### ¹⁴³ bolsopaseo

# bolsp**o**pase**o.**

"Bolso" means bag, "paseo" means to stroll.

The project "bolsopaseo" literally ties to one another not only pieces of leather, it just as much interlinks different cultures.

As a matter of course it all started with a stroll. Traveling through Central America the fascination on seeing how handicrafts are done with existing materials and machines in most imaginative and resourceful ways made a lasting impression on the European mind.

By making use of the inventive potential in the exchange of European ideas and Central American skills, it was possible to design an everyday article – such as a bag — with an unexpected fresh approach, giving the product on one hand the authenticity of traditional craftsmanship on the other the contemporary design without frills.

This quality is reflected in the design of the logo. Alluding to an imaginary walk a thin diagonal line connects the two words "bolso" and "paseo" in the logo. The diagonal of that line is part of the corporate design and can be found in all the applications.

Being a strong graphic element it opens a wide range of uses without losing recognition value. The logo's simplicity and variable possibilities of application and its elaboration in questions regarding detail speak the same language as the bags.

The corporate design of "bolsopaseo" has grown simultaneously to the bag assortment. Where at the beginning only a folded flyer was produced, over time there have been added more printed matters.

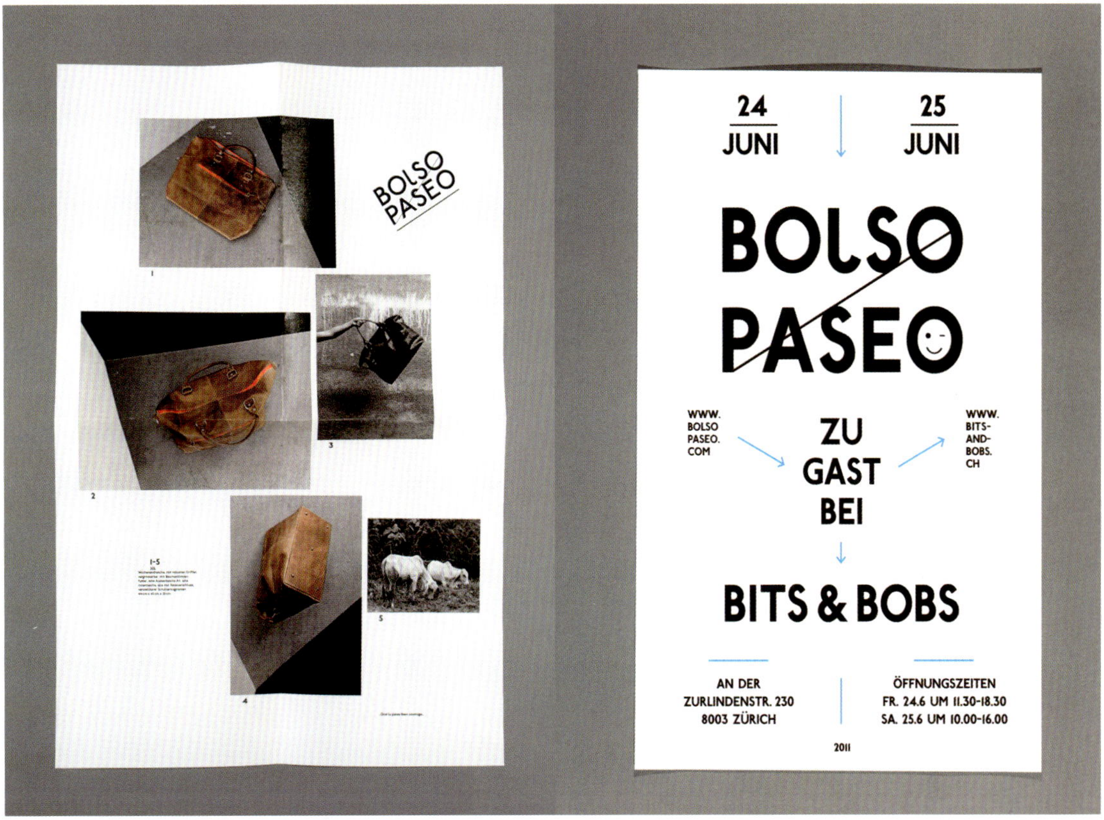

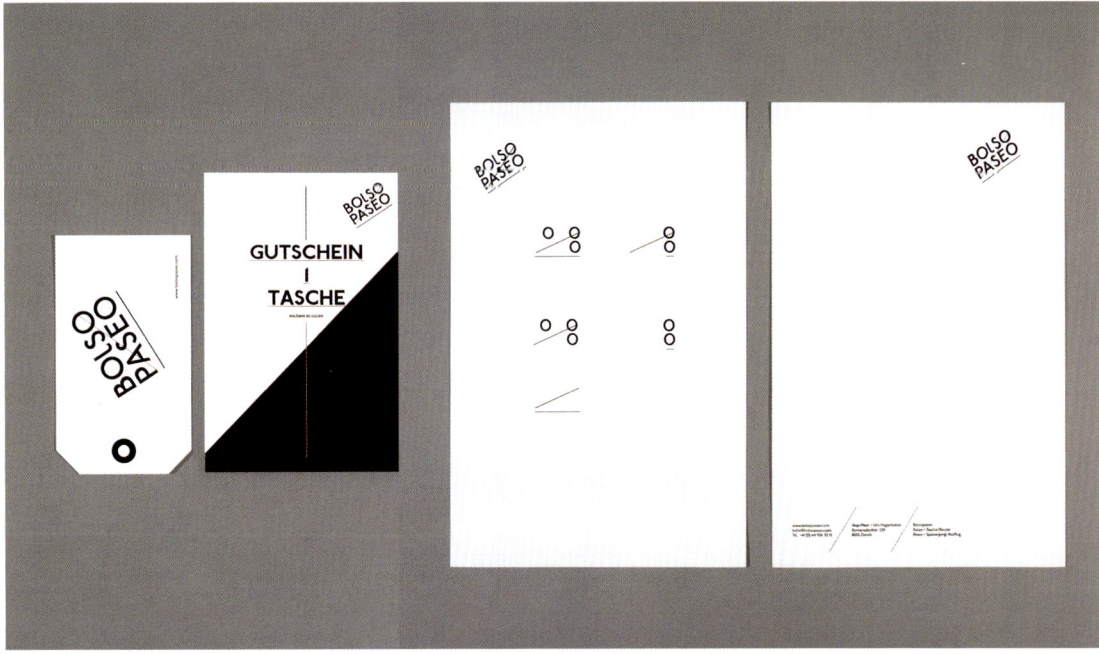

:Similar Difference

144 Dethier Architectures

# Daniel Dethier & Associés

# Dethier Architectures

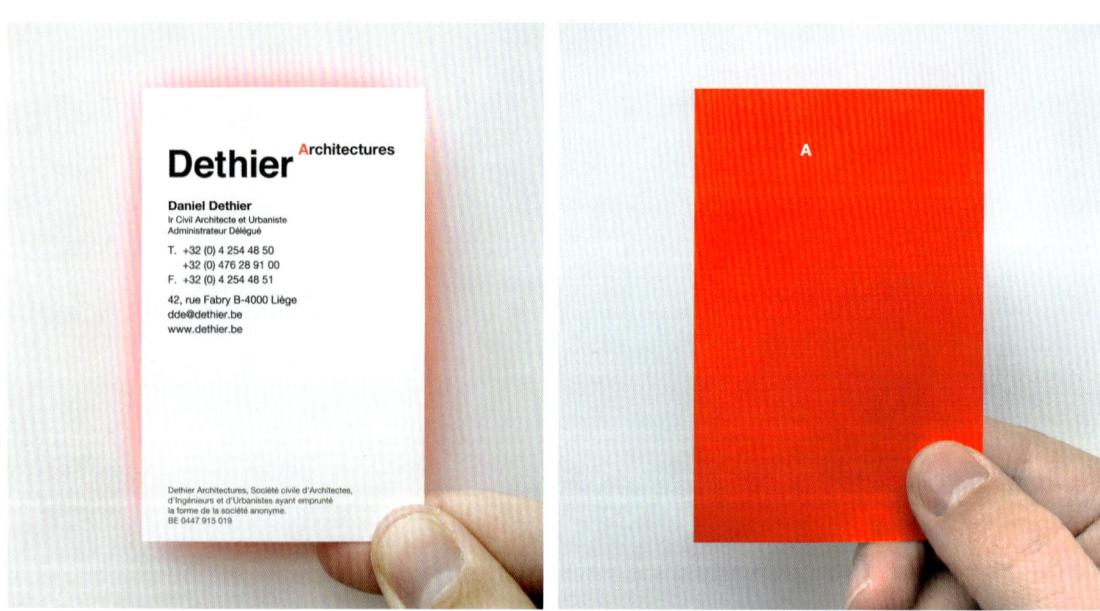

144
:Client's Brief
The aim was to refresh the logo from "Dethier & Associés" to "Dethier Architectures".

:Design Philosophy
"The simpler the better" was the design philosophy We Love Moules Frites obeyed during the whole developing process.

:Similar Difference

145 Made By Humans

made by humans          made by humans

146 Tine Kozjak

          TINEKOZJAK

147 Maria Pinto

MARIAPINTO          MARIAPINTO™

---

145
:Client's Brief
The aim was to subtly enhance the existing logo by more effectively communicating the essence of the brand; based on the company's history of initial hand made products and its contemporary aesthetic.

:Design Philosophy
Cameron Snelgar removed the serifs to symbolize sticks, one of the first materials that humans used to make things and reversed the "s" to signify that the logo was made by humans.

146
:Client's Brief
The new logo shall be theatrical, inspired by the darkness and its mystics.

:Design Philosophy
The rebrand project finally graduated from concept to form, from dark to light, from stiff to airy.

147
:Client's Brief
Maria Pinto is a fashion designer from Chicago. The new logo and identity was need for the launch of her first boutique in Chicago.

:Design Philosophy
The idea of the logo came from her design aesthetic of using strong construction with the delicate materials. The thinner weight of the san-serif typeface was carefully chosen and based on. The customized version of the final logo reflects both qualities of her work.

:Similar Difference

148 Fantastic Norway Architects

148
:Client's Brief
The architecture company became known for driving around Norway with a red caravan, bringing architecture discussions into many small villages. The new logo should make reference to the red caravan and communicate a sharp, professional, innovative but still a friendly and accessible architecture office.

:Design Philosophy
The idea was to create a simpler and iconified version of the caravan instead of a detailed drawing. Renata Barros and her partners chose the symbol used in road signage, which also related to "being on the move". The simple, straightforward font was applied to every material and the simplicity of the icon allows it to be used as background patterns or as a dominant element.

:Similar Difference

:Similar Difference

149 VdpArchitecten

uǝʇɔǝʇᴉɥɔɹⱯdp∇rchitecten

VdpArchitecten

149
:Client's Brief
VdpArchitects (formerly Van Dam & Partners Architects) is a young achitectual firm in the Netherlands. In addition to architecture, VdpArchitects also does interior architecture and product design.

:Design Philosophy
Construction drawings can be used to stand out. Besides Buro Reng designed a custom typeface for building plans and presentations. When used in coding of construction drawings the typography forms a recognizable part of the corporate identity.

:Similar Difference

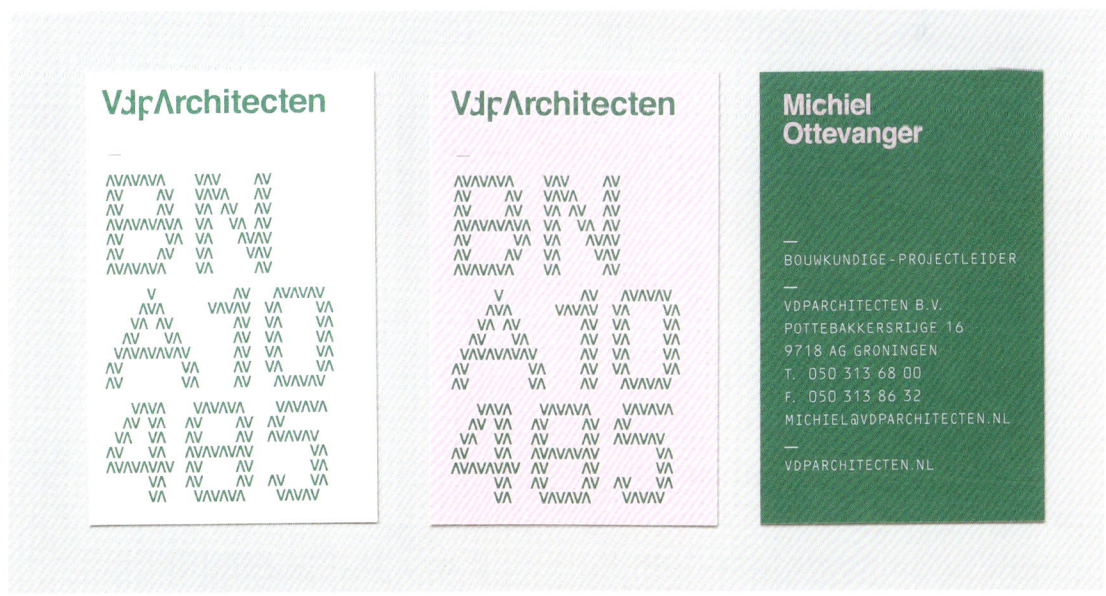

:Similar Difference

150 Penduka Namibia

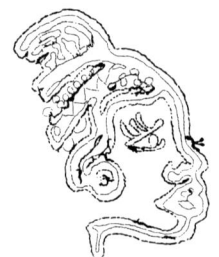

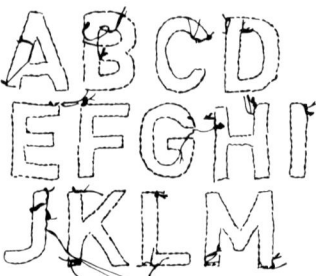

---

150
:Client's Brief
Penduka is a non-governmental development organization working with women in Namibia. By purchasing a Penduka product you do not just have a beautiful and unique product for yourself, but you also contribute towards a better life for women in Namibia.

:Design Philosophy
Penduka women embroider their stories using typical imagery of the ethnic groups they originate from. Commissioned by Buro Reng the women of Penduka also embroidered letters and icons on cotton. Buro Reng used this to create a website, a custom typeface and the logo for Penduka.

:Similar Difference

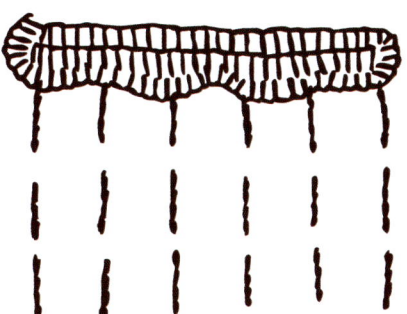

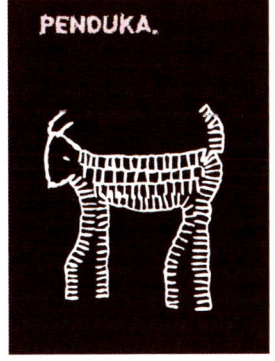

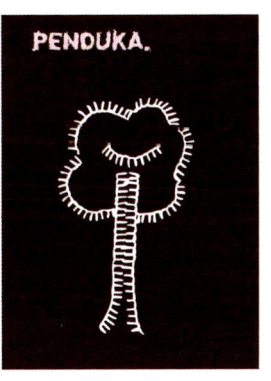
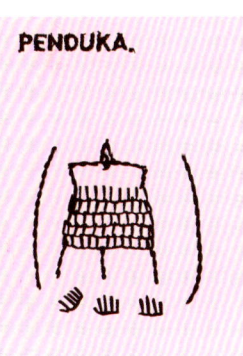

:Similar Difference

151 New Readymade Projects

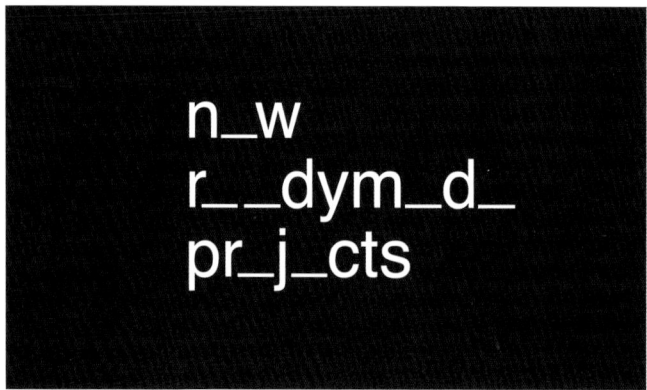

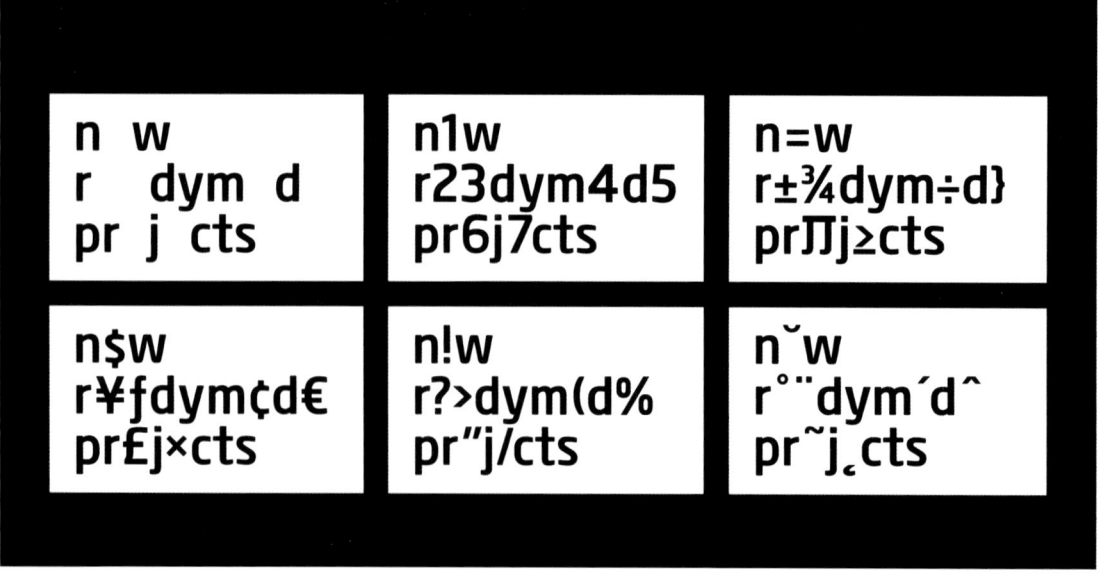

151
:Client's Brief
New Readymade Projects wanted to redesign the studio's logo to give it more impact and strength.

:Design Philosophy
Alex Lin built on the idea of the exclusion of vowels and came up with a set of logos, each one with the vowels replaced by a set of glyphs.

:Similar Difference

152 Mittongtare Studio

153 Vassdal & Eriksen

152
National advertising and editorial clients have used Pornchai Mittongtare's elegant images to showcase food, still life, consumer products and lifestyle to a wide audience over the last 10 years. TomTor Studio helped them to restyle their brand identity.

153
:Client's Brief
The aim was to position Vassdal & Eriksen as the accountants for the creative industry, through it's visual identity.

:Design Philosophy
Haltenbanken combined mathematical accuracy with humourous illutrations.

125

:Overturn

01 Shine

02 Water For People

03 Worldreader

01
:Client's Brief
Shine wanted to simplify a complicated and dated hand-drawn logo mark for a successful London PR agency.

:Design Philosophy
After a long development process, the eventual solution was the most simple representation of a shining sun possible, applied to print collateral in a variety if different reflective finishes.

02
Water For People, a nonprofit organization, promotes safe drinking water and sanitation projects in developing countries. The brand identity was designed to reflect Water For People's vision of a world in which all people have access to clean water. It's about education and collaboration and iteration with governments, villages and corporations; the strength of one person working with another until communities around the world witness the water crisis wash away under the strength of their efforts — a current of change.

03
:Client's Brief
Worldreader is an American nonprofit, public charity involved in developing and delivering e-reader technology, providing access to books for children in developing countries. They needed a brand strategy which could be self-explanatory of the initiative and capable of communicating on a very emotional level.

:Design Philosophy
The identity is built around "reading", therefore the use of type. Simple use of colour allows text to turn into images, creating a strong and ownable system. The logo morphology recalls a child reading and a blooming flower, transmitting positivity and hope.

:Overturn

04 Conservation International

04
:Client's Brief
Conservation International is one of the most influential environmental groups in the world, successfully protecting half a billion acres of wilderness. To broaden its appeal, CI is redefining its mission, focusing on humankind's reliance on nature. The organization needed a mark that would match its new message.

:Design Philosophy
A simple blue circle underlined with green symbolizes our blue planet — emphasized, supported, and sustained — as well as a unique human form.

:Overturn

### 05  9/11 Memorial Museum

**What did your client hope to achieve through redesigning the logo?**

We were tasked with creating a new shorthand name (at the time our client was using their legal name, "National September 11 Memorial and Museum at the World Trade Center," which was too lengthy and problematic in applications), a new logo and a new visual system.

Our goal was to create a new identity that accurately reflects the events and emotions of the day, is easy to use, and communicates hope and remembrance.

**The collaboration of black and blue makes people feel silent and melancholy. Is it the reason why you employed them as the theme colors of the new logo?**

The colors were deliberately selected to convey a sense of solemnity, austerity, and hope: The blue represents the space in the sky where the towers once stood and, when used on black, suggests hope in a time of darkness.

**"11" in the logo looks like WTC Twin Towers. Is it the original intention of yours?**

Indeed. Combining the date with the building silhouettes creates an indelible connection in people's minds — they are a powerful, unmistakable symbol of that day's events.

**What did you consider when redesigning the logo?**

We considered a variety of factors during the development of the identity, anything from the color of the sky that day to the absolute horror of the day's events, as well as the sense of hope, resilience, and national pride felt in the aftermath. We wanted to create an identity that would properly honor the victims and educate future generations.

**As 9-11 is a disaster not only to the U.S.A. but also the whole world, are you under great pressure during the redesigned process and even after the new logo's promulgation?**

This is a project to which everyone — internationally, nationally, and, of course, locally in New York — feels connected. We wanted to help further their cause and honor the victims.

:Overturn

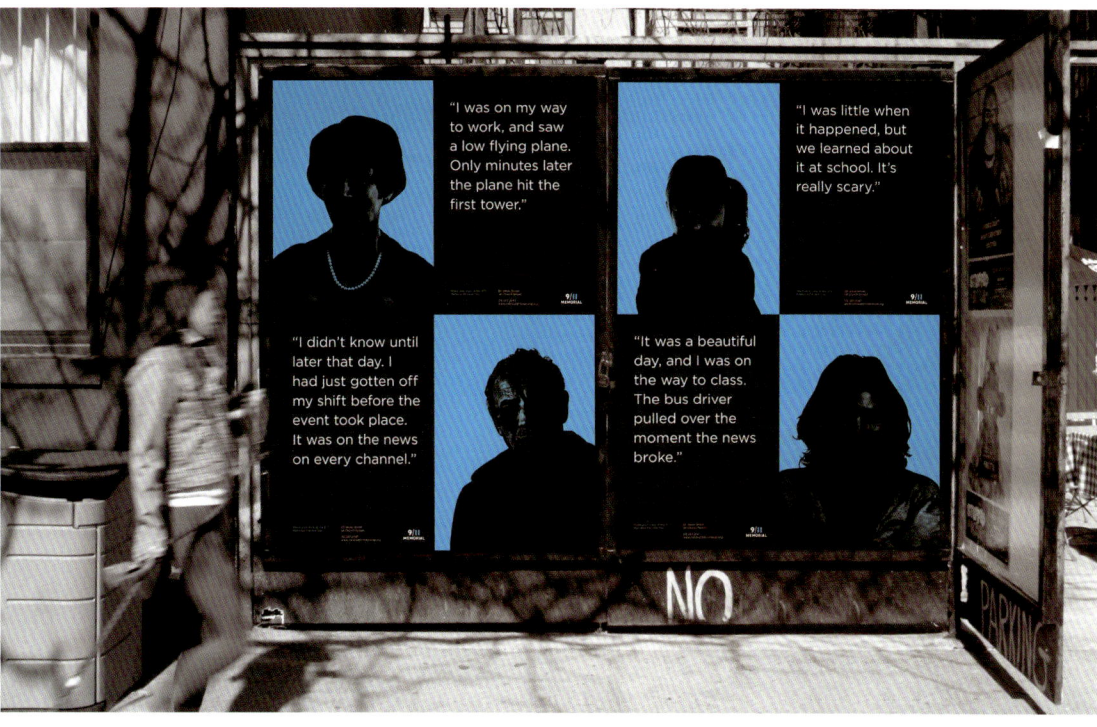

:Overturn

06 Blood in Blood out

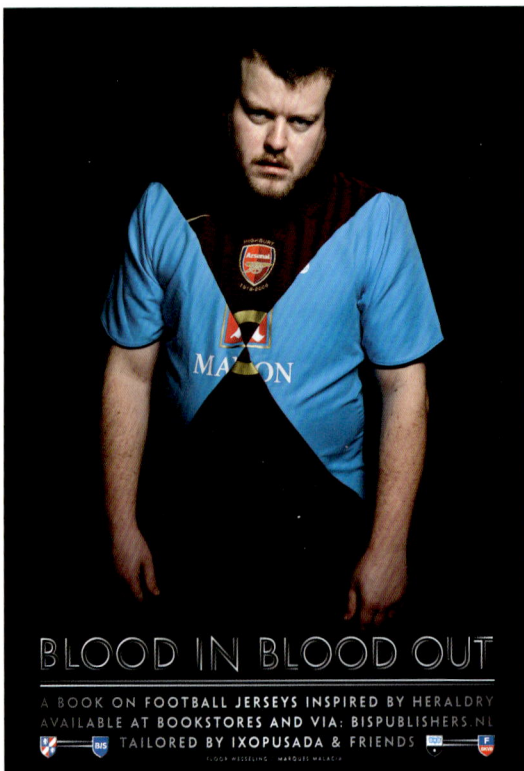
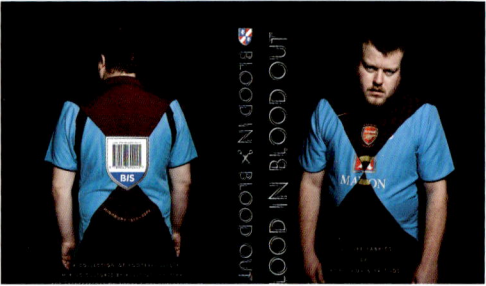
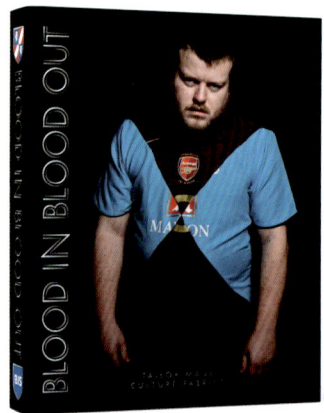

06
:Client's Brief

Blood In Blood Out wanted a logo for project about combining football jerseys according to the rules of heraldry.

:Design Philosophy

Floor Wesseling made the logo classic but also modern, and restyled to black background because of the portraits on black.

:Overturn

07 Matías Nadal. Composer

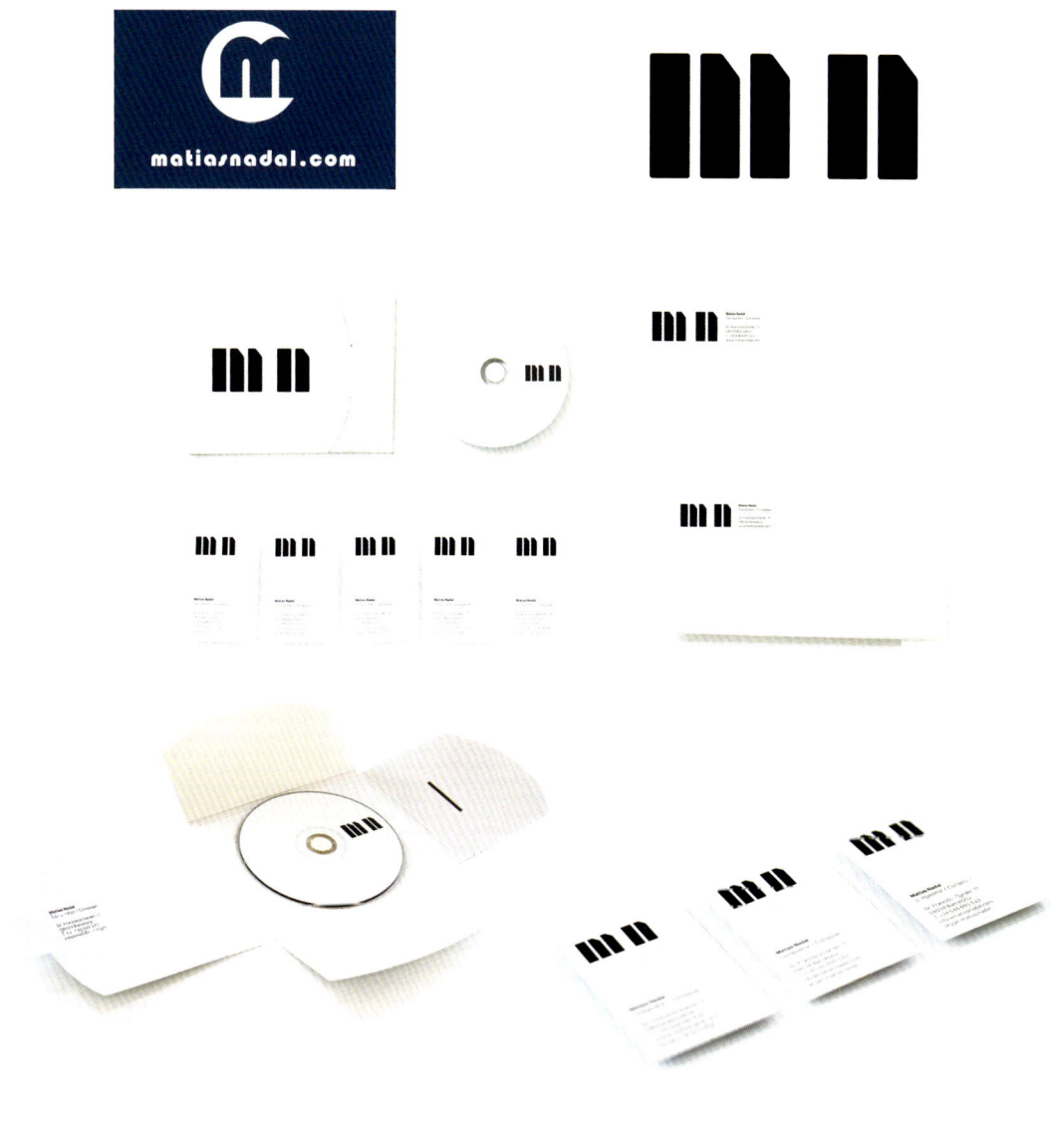

07
:Client's Brief
A modern logo was wanted, with limited budget and trend-free visual identity for a music composer working in film, advertising, television and diverse artistic projects.

:Design Philosophy
The logotype is constructed with Matías Nadal's initials in stencil, MN, which form the black keys of a music keyboard, his main tool for expression. Repeating the symbol five times a whole keyboard was generated.

:Similar Difference

141 Anthony-And

**ANTHONY-AND**

142 Sara Merz Photography

**SARA MERZ FOTOGRAFIE**

---

141
:Client's Brief
Anthony-And is a hairdresser in Brussels. Its first visual identity was based on the title in basic Helvetica-black-extended font.

:Design Philosophy
When entrusted with the project, OBLIQUE drew a type inspired by lots of hair on the floor after a haircut. Some parts of the round letters were cut while preserving the readability of the logo.

142
:Client's Brief
Sara Merz Photography asked for a new logo as simple as the old one keeping the Helvet font.

:Design Philosophy
We Love Moules Frites created a kind of hand-drawn photogram.

:Overturn

08 Cricket Victoria

09 Tasmania

10 Fire Services

08
The confidence of "the big V" positions Victoria as the premier Australian cricketing state. Dynamic stripes represent the MCG, the home of cricket in Victoria, the team of 11 players, the green turf of the local ground and the international horizons the game of cricket can reach.

09
The Brand Tasmania mark is derived from the inspiring natural landscapes of Tasmania. Its precise and effortless form reflects the pure quality of Tasmanian craftmanship, produce and services.

The shape of the logo is derived from a stylised map of Tasmania, an icon recognised by a global audience.

10
The central driver is unity, of change, of bringing together strengths, experience, differences and similarities toward one goal and as one team. The colours are born from the principles of organization (collective, integrated, pulling together as one), service (fire services and services to the community) and danger (the environment that our people work in).

:Overturn

11 Swisscom

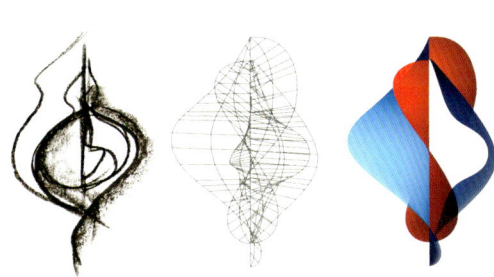

11
:Client's Brief
Moving Brands was engaged to create an identity that expressed the vision of the company, which was an increased customer orientation and expansion from telecoms and IT to media and entertainment sectors.

:Design Philosophy
It was important that the mark was both "fixed and flexible," with the hard line of the axis working with the malleable, dynamic curves. Each gradient, pixel and point was studied and measured to determine how it would look, but just as importantly how it would behave.

Although the brandmark is a dynamic, moving identity, there is a distinct brandmark which is used on print and static communications. The type compliments and mimics both the straight axis, and the curvature of the life form, as seen in the "l" and "m".

:Overturn

12 Shot

13 Comédie De Reims

14 The Consortium for Street Children

12
:Client's Brief
Shot is a company dedicated to web design and development. They wanted to show in their logo high level of design.

:Design Philosophy
MANIFIESTO FUTURA decided to made their own typography for this project, that at the same time could function as an icon.

13
:Client's Brief
Comédie De Reims wanted to have a logo based on the architecture of the theatre building. It had to show the contemporary and new aspects of the place.

:Design Philosophy
The shapes intersect to give birth to a simple and strong elliptic form with a central composition. Red as for the theatre seat and curtain's velvet.

14
:Client's Brief
The Consortium for Street Children is the leading international network dedicated to promoting the rights of street-involved children. By acting together as a group with a collective strength, their aim is to reach wider audiences with a greater voice.

:Design Philosophy
To help CSC communicate more effectively, build awareness of their brand and enable them to connect with their target audiences, Purpose have developed a powerful identity and visual language for the organisation based around the core thought "Amplifier" and giving children a voice.

:Overturn

15 Coca-Cola Freestyle

16 Creative Auiance of New Orleans

15
:Client's Brief
The Coca-Cola Freestyle logo represents the new fountain beverage experience developed by The Coca-Cola Company, which offers 125 drink brands at the touch of a few buttons.

:Design Philosophy
The friendliness and simplicity of the Coca-Cola Freestyle logo character and type help make the technology approachable and build recognition of the machine as a Coca-Cola offering. The cup held within the logo is formed from the shape of the trademarked Coca-Cola Bell Glass, which further strengthens the brand communication.

16
:Client's Brief
Creative Auiance of New Orleans required freshening up the look of this non-profit arts organization. It does not even read as – CANO, but moreso, CAN.

:Design Philosophy
This small town look was elevated to be an international style with simple geometries. And bright colors is able to attract the interest of international artists to its arts organization.

:Overturn

## [17] BB's

**What does your client hope to achieve through redesigning the logo?**

The client needed to achieve an improvement in sales and attract a younger, more affluent customer base.

**The new logo is totally different from the old one. Why did you abandon everything of the old logo and design a brand new one?**

The brand needed to radically upgrade every aspect of its offer. The logo is of course the tip of the iceberg. Every single aspect was looked at. We always said that unless the offer was improved then they are wasting their money on a "rebrand", people are not stupid.

A Barista is on board training the staff, so they have great coffee, the sandwiches are no longer piled high in the counter displays and the muffins, now with new ingredients, are smaller and more delectable than the enormous things they once were.

The first "new look" UK store to open, is week on week trading between 32% + 51% up compared to last year, so it goes without saying that we have one very happy client. The old identity had no brand value, so we had nothing to lose.

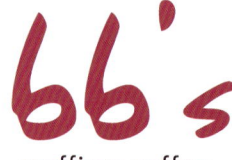

**Black looks cold while magenta looks so vivacious. But when they are collocated with each other, a certain sense of fashion is generated. Why did you employ black and magenta as the theme colors of the logo instead of red of the previous one?**

Red is so common in food retail and although BB's had used it for many years, we wanted to depart radically from where they were and "own" our own colour. Black is a good base, it allows the magenta to "sing" and it makes the muffins stand out, and like the little black dress, everything looks good in it.

**You use lowercase letters instead of capital letters in the new logo. What do you think the difference between these two types of letters in the perspective of design? Why did you apply lowercase letters in this project?**

We wanted an informality to the brand, and with our "muffin moments ®" we wanted the customer to take ownership of the brand. Sometimes a whisper is louder than a wolf whistle.

**You have tried out some other different typeface when developing the new logo. Could you tell us why did you choose this typeface in the final selecting?**

The final font/logo chosen was most suited and related to the new concept of the brand and its customers. It feels new, contemporary and is easy to spot amidst a crowd.

Because it's your birthday • because the sky is blue • because that gorgeous stranger smiled at you again • because you have a new job and your desk has a lovely view • because I got the kids to school on time today • because I'm sorry • because it's a girl • because it's a boy • because because because • because I love you • because your diet starts tomorrow • because it's raining • because you have a cold • because you passed • because it's only an exam • because it's my birthday • because it's Monday • because it's a leap year • because it's Friday • because I can still do a cart wheel • because it's a beautiful day • because it's a cloudy day • because because because • because it's your birthday • because the sky is blue • because that gorgeous stranger smiled at you again • because any excuse will do

bb's
coffee • muffins

:Overturn

18 KURA Restaurant

18
:Client's Brief
Kura is a Japanese-fusion restaurant based in Hollywood, California. Anti/Anti was brought in to find and extract the restaurant's "story", while also creating a unified branding experience from outdoor signage to take-out menu.

:Design Philosophy
Anti/Anti redesigned the Kura logo to strongly associate with a traditional Japanese storehouse (the literal translation of Kura) aesthetic, while still being contemporary and inviting. The new logo is able to communicate the craft and history of Japan, while clearly positioning Kura within the upscale culinary offerings in Los Angeles.

:Overturn

19 Wolfgang Puck

Wolfgang Puck

20 Restaurant Natália

21 Moku

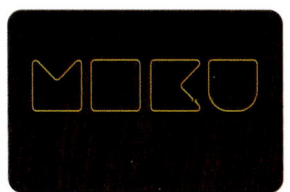

### 19
**:Client's Brief**

Known for some of the world's finest restaurants, Wolfgang Puck had begun to build a business that would allow more people to enjoy his tasty recipes everyday.

**:Design Philosophy**

Duffy & Partners designed a brand language that celebrates the quality and artistry of Wolfgang's creations; signals taste and wellness; and captures the passion of the man behind the brand.

### 20
**:Client's Brief**

Restaurante Natália was 24 and wanted to update its image. Sober and elegant design intended to convey the history and philosophy of the restaurant.

**:Design Philosophy**

The creative process was characterized by a personalized approach based on research and concepts specific to the project. To combine the strengths of this restaurant, such as tradition, history and modernity was the main job.

### 21
**:Client's Brief**

Moku means "wood" in Japanese.

**:Design Philosophy**

DTM_INC always starts out making a logo in black and white. DTM_INC believes that if it doesn't work in black and white it will never work in color.

:Overturn

22 Europharm

23 Applegate

24 Loteria De Catalunya

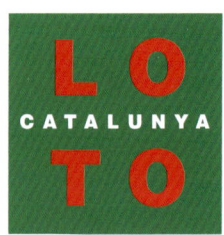 

22
:Client's Brief
The take-over of Europharm by GlaxoSmithKline (GSK), the leader of pharma market in Romania, has marked a turning point for the Romanian company and the premise for a new internal and external brand identity.

:Design Philosophy
The new logo, whose outline implies a symbolic heart, retained the colour and the symbolic element (the serpent) associated with Europharm but also hinted subtly at GSK's family of forms.

23
:Client's Brief
Evolve the existing Applegate Farms branding to transition the brand from niche to mass market and reinforce the brand's philosophy of "taste, truth and trust".

:Design Philosophy
The job was to help Applegate Farms change the way American eats meat; one slice at a time. The name of Applegate was simplified. Taste, truth and trust are represented by the symbol of an arrow piercing the heart of an apple. The naive styling of the icon captures the family spirit of the brand.

24
:Client's Brief
Loteria De Catalunya required redefining the brand design to strengthen its differential identification.

:Design Philosophy
Lucky, fun, new personality, catalan were all the key words involved in the redesigning process.

## [25] Chicken Pecker

**What are the client's requests for redesigning the logo?**

Redesigning the logo was our idea, not the client's request. Originally, they requested us to redesign the menu. However, we proposed to redesign not only the menu, but also the logo and other related visual matters.

**The new logo is totally different from the old one. Why did you abandon everything from the old logo and design a brand new one?**

The old logo did not have a clear concept grounded in what they wanted to represent. Considering how the restaurant needs to appear and how it should be, we redesigned the logo based on the concept of a "Japanese countryside restaurant specializing in chicken."

**Green always represents something fresh. Please explain your idea of applying green as the theme color of the new logo.**

This restaurant serves deep fried chicken, grills, hamburgers, and bowls of rice. Everything was brown. We chose green because it is vivid and fresh, and produces a succulent feeling that is well matched to brown.

**Did you encounter any challenges while designing the new logo?**

We needed to work around the restrictions. We were unable to reconstruct the environment, such as the restaurant interior and signage. Instead of constructing it from the beginning, we were challenged to get close to ideal with such constraints.

**What do you and your client think of the end result?**

By applying the new logo to all aspects of the restaurant, the logo reinforced the brand image through consistency and helped to create a new identity for the restaurant. This means that Chicken Pecker was able to increase brand recognition as a specialty restaurant for chicken dishes. It is a treasured and well-established restaurant, and it became famous for its memorable chicken signage. Our client is very satisfied with the result.

:Overturn

:Overturn

:Overturn

:Overturn

## [26] Marmalade Toast

**The new logo didn't inherit any elements of the previous logo. Why did you abandon everything of the previous logo and develop a totally new one?**

The choice to redesign from a clean slate was a result we made wishing to include "Marmalade" as both the headline and the co-branding element. As the café was previously known as "Toast", the inclusion of "Marmalade" meant that an entirely new rebranding approach was possible. Also, by doing so, it was a strategic move on to the end to create greater kinship among the café, the café's management, Marmalade Group, and the sister restaurant, The Marmalade Pantry.

**Black and white are two never outdated colors. And they are always collocated with each other. You employed them as the theme colors of the new logo. Why did you use them?**

The colour scheme was to keep classic and unadorned, better differentiating Marmalade Toast from its previous identity. The former brandmark employed pastel pink to create a semblance of cupcakes, which the café is famed for. However, as the café expanded its offerings and began attracting a more upmarket consumer base, the decision to adopt a timeless identity was more apparent.

**The characters of the new logo are set vertically, which is seldom seen in logo design. What inspired you to create the new logo like this?**

The inspiration was derived from the tiers of a sandwich, which meant it was conceptually sound for the letters in "Toast" to be set vertically.

**What's the concept of cutting the bottom of every character in the logo by the lines?**

We wanted the brandmark to be visually reminiscent of slices of bread popping out of a toaster. Slightly rounded-off corners at the bottom of the letters that merge into the lines suggests melted cheese on toast.

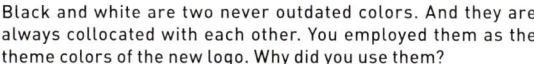

27 JamFactory

27
:Client's Brief
As galleries, studios and shops, JamFactory represents the best of design and craftsmanship, nurturing and showcasing talent, educating and inspiring the public. Their visual identity, of course, had to speak to design.

:Design Philosophy
The new logo, in its geometry and line weight, recalls the creative process, drawing blueprints and planning. Its level of customisation sets it apart, making it unique and distinctive.

:Overturn

28 Pizzeria Delfina

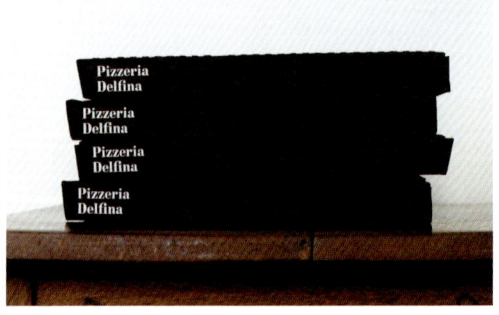

28
:Client's Brief
Redesigning the visual identity, capturing the guiding philosophy of Casual Perfection were what Pizzeria Delfina exactly needed. And brand personality traits are neapolitan, whimsical, relaxed and honest.

:Design Philosophy
The challenge of visualizing Casual Perfection was answered by creating an iconic hand-drawn mark, paired with a strong wordmark and a bold colour palette.

29 Gelati Sky

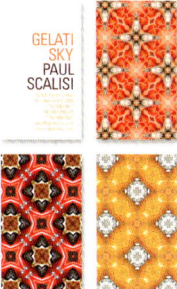

29

Gelati Sky is a boutique, premium gelati range. The story of Gelati Sky was based around Gelati Sky's founder Paul Scalisi Memories of Rome, eating gelati. Truly Deeply created visuals that were strikingly unique, representing his story and sparked conversation. The communication platform "it's what dreams taste like" was derived from the brand strategy definition. The concept combined imagery of Italy with objects that represented the flavors creating a unique, organic and scrumptious shape for each flavor. The packaging looks like memories and dreams of Italy,

The packaging was the strongest step to build a brand consumers could connect with. The package needed to not only reflect the personality and story but also to look different while still maintaining premium feel. The taste of the gelati is simply amazing. And it would be very successful that a rich, beautiful label which would get buyers and customers excited is developed.

:Overturn

30 Griffin Theatre Company

  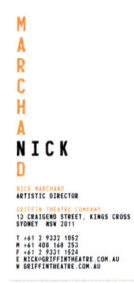  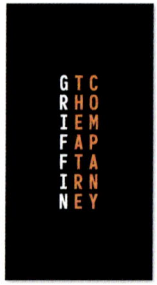

 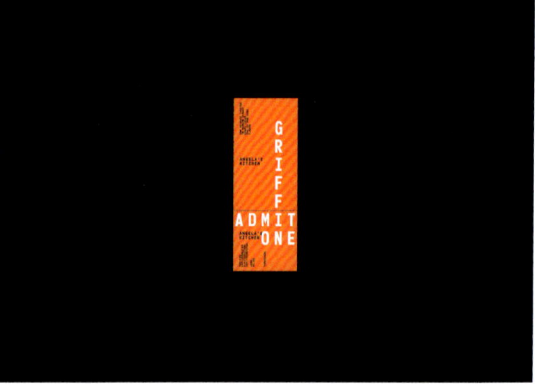

### :Client's Brief

For the past 30 years, the team at Griffin have been able to bring together the most talented and creative people to make groundbreaking theatre. But in stark contrast, they have not been able to present themselves in a way that reflects the highly acclaimed quality of the work they produce.

### :Design Philosophy

The brand responds to the emotional highs and lows of each play through the metaphor of "the deep end", and with an identity that allows Griffin to express its own creativity and personality through words presented as a matrix. The brand identity itself is rooted in language. Typography and wordplay intertwine to create myriad interpretations.

:Overturn

31 Life Uncommon Photography

32 The Islands of the Bahamas

33 BTO

---

**31**
**:Client's Brief**
The new logo needed to accentuate the photographer's editorial-style photography.

**:Design Philosophy**
Design Ranch drew attention to the unique details in the moments captured in David Tsai's photographs.

**32**
**:Client's Brief**
Bahamas needed an entirely new brand identity, one that not only made the country stand apart, but also was flexible for many different constituencies to use.

**:Design Philosophy**
The concept was designing a stylized map of the Bahamas — an identity system to highlight each of the 14 major tourist destinations and their many unique offerings.

**33**
**:Client's Brief**
The aim was to reposition the organisation through a new visual identity.

**:Design Philosophy**
The symbol is a visual representation of the creation of growth through science, new technology and ground breaking research.

:Overturn

34 Tassimo

35 Meredith

36 Aster

---

### 34
**:Client's Brief**
Turner Duckworth was briefed to bring the brand to life by communicating its unique point of difference in this crowded sector. Tassimo offers the consumer premium branded choice of great coffees and more from brands consumers know and love.

**:Design Philosophy**
The new identity system works across many touch points from retail packs, at home dispenser packs, POS, CRM and online applications. The power brand Tassimo leads with the T disk shape allowing the partner brand opportunity to express their attributes. A complex system made simple through clever design.

### 35
**:Client's Brief**
Meredith is one of the nation's leading media and marketing corporations. While Meredith's corporate brand and business groups (publishing and broadcasting) spoke to legacy distribution channels and competencies, they did not capture 1) the dynamic; 2) the media brands consumers trust every day; or 3) the strength of Meredith's marketing solutions.

**:Design Philosophy**
The brand positioning strategy is "Engaging Lives". The updated corporate logo featured four interlaced letter "m's" that reflect both Meredith's ability to distribute content across multiple platforms, its significant marketing capabilities, and also communicate Meredith's brand values and culture.

### 36
**:Client's Brief**
Aster, one of the oldest shoe brands in France, has been delivering high quality children's footwear since 1913. As its products have been copied a lot by its competitors, Aster wanted to strengthen its brand identity and awareness.

**:Design Philosophy**
BAYADERES upgraded the shoe's unique die-cut shape (the Aster flower) to new brand icon status, establishing a greater link between brand and product. In this case, the connection is mutually beneficial, increasing memorability of the logo and distinctiveness of the shoes.

:Overturn

37 Patria

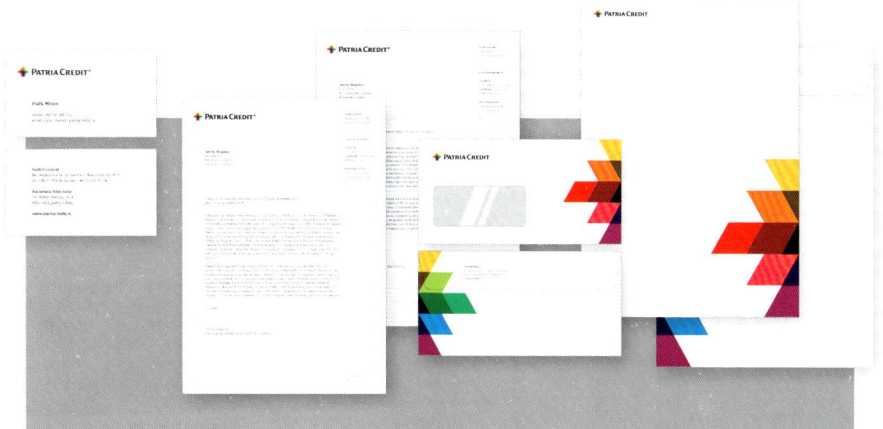

37
:Client's Brief
CAPA Finance was a micro-credit agency that grew to be one of the largest non-banking institutions specialized in micro-financing in Romania. Facing fierce competition from banks, in 2008 the company received EBRD as a joint shareholder and decided to reinforce its market position.

:Design Philosophy
The new name, Patria (Romanian for "homeland") and the vivid graphic symbol, inspired by Romanian popular motifs and Brancusi's Endless Column, stand for hope, life, optimism and familiarity, while bringing into the current life a metaphor immanent in the Romanian's collective imagery.

:Overturn

38 Bresciani Cover All

39 Avia

40 HTC

38
:Client's Brief
Bresciani Cover All signed a sponsorship deal with Brescia Calcio SpA for the 2009/2010 football season. After that, the brand stood on the uniforms on the chest. So a new logo was needed.

:Design Philosophy
Branding and communications agency Raineri Design helped Bresciani Cover All to design their new logo. The new logo is a cover, large enough to contain even a star, which symbolizes that which exists in the highest of human dreams.

39
:Client's Brief
Aviat Networks is a provider of end-to-end wireless solutions to clients that include public and private telecom operators in countries all across the globe.

:Design Philosophy
The new corporate logo focuses on the point of connection between two networks. This icon is also a symbol for the idea of connecting businesses and communities to each other across the globe.

40
:Client's Brief
HTC asked Figtree to develop a strong brand positioning and identity to give them a differentiated position in an increasingly crowded market.

:Design Philosophy
The outcome was based around the idea of "quietly brilliant"; a simple, powerful and meaningful attitude, one that really reflects who HTC are and what they believe. The personality, visual identity and values Figtree developed all stemmed from this core idea.

:Overturn

41 CareerBliss

41
:Client's Brief
CareerBliss is a new company with a very distinctive approach. They invite people to look at their employment options based on how happy they might be working at that particular company. This idea is fun and unique... And it immediately put a smile on people's face.

:Design Philosophy
The logo is a combination of two simple concepts: "work" and "happiness". "Work" is represented by a file folder which is a ubiquitous item found in virtually any work setting worldwide; while "happiness" is represented by a smiling face. Really, the idea and the identity could not be simpler... Yet it could not do the job better.

:Overturn

42 Syfy

43 Sygma Bank

44 Savana

42
:Client's Brief
Syfy TV channel approached Proud Creative with the name change already a large part of their strategic thinking. Syfy — unlike "Sci Fi" — establishes an ownable trademark; unique to the brand.

:Design Philosophy
Proud Creative retained the positive associations of the genre, whilst embracing the possibilities of imagination. The logo appears almost as a "blank canvas" – ready for whatever your creativity can throw at it.

43
:Client's Brief
Sygma Bank decided to become a first-choice brand in modern consumer finance branch. Connection with Cetelem Bank was catalyst of changes. The new brand is supposed to be based on the following brand pillars: good value for price, availability and accessibility, simplicity and product personality.

:Design Philosophy
Innovative and unique system of visual identification was adapted to multiple channels of communications. Design was coming beyond banking category draft, emphasized simplicity, no distance and positive approach to the customer.

44
:Client's Brief
The paint creator Fabryo Corporation has redefined the product portfolio and decided to redesign its premium brand Savana in order to consolidate the brand's position on an increasingly competitive market.

:Design Philosophy
The old identity was rather suggesting dryness, coarseness, and was not credible in communicating the quality attribute. The new visual identity was designed so as to keep on supporting the name but also to inspire quality through life, color and exuberance, by the use of animal illustration.

:Overturn

45 Reddingsbrigade

46 MyDesign

45
:Client's Brief
It was time for the Dutch lifesavingbrigade to freshen up their identity. The new logo had to fit in with the logo of the Dutch police and firebrigade, and be less cluttered than the original.

:Design Philosophy
The hexagon shape is loosely based on the shape of a coat of arms. Within this shape there are two elements that build the logo. First, the waves, and secondly, the orange striping as it appears on the boats and other vehicles of the brigade.

46
:Client's Brief
MyDesign / Mylonadis offers industrial and interior design solutions. They asked to refresh their identity.

:Design Philosophy
The identity is minimalistic. The symbol of the logo is cut out in order to reveal the materials being used by the designer. For each application a different image or material is revealed underneath.

:Overturn

47 Regional Arts Victoria

48 Qval

49 DTM Inc

47
:Client's Brief

The main goal in designing Regional Arts Victoria's rebrand, was to create a mark that set them apart from corporate partners and clearly defined them as an innovative arts based organization.

:Design Philosophy

The redesigned brandmark reflects RAV's vision of connecting artists with communities across Victoria.

48
:Client's Brief

As Quist Valuation becomes Qval, they needed to create the logo for online tool that allows companies and investors to centralize, organize and analyze data in a secure environment, enabling the generation of powerful insights into their businesses.

:Design Philosophy

The solution was to develop a symbol composed of two circles, reminiscent of a Q, and communicating with simplicity that from micro to macro, all data lives within the power of Qval. The online nature of the offering is conveyed through a vibrant orange and the geometric, all-lowercase wordmark.

49
:Client's Brief

DTM_INC wanted to make the logo typographic.

:Design Philosophy

DTM_INC always starts out making logos in black and white, believing that if it doesn't work in black and white it will never work in color.

:Overturn

50 Arema

51 Global Encounters

50
:Client's Brief
Arema is the largest political party of Madagascar, founded in 1976 by former president Didier Ratsiraka. The party needed a fresher and more modern look, and to get rid of all communism related iconography that didn't represent the party's current philosophy, mostly focusing on democracy, "green", sustainability and federalism.

:Design Philosophy
The new identity is conceived as a modular system built around a base module: the triangle, directional symbol of the dynamism and changes required by the country. The structure of the party's logo translates visually the new party positioning and the will of the country for radical changes.

51
:Client's Brief
Global Encounters is a destination management company operating in the tourism sector, specialized in Latin America. The industry is segmented by client typologies, and by services. The organization has grown in different parts of the business but lacked a distinctive positioning on the market.

:Design Philosophy
The brand strategy has looked at the business as two-fold, B2B and B2C. The first step consisted of establishing a corporate brand that helped establish a unique positioning, reinterpreting cultural elements in a more contemporary spirit. The architecture has defined the sub-brands for each business unit; the summation of these, shapes the mother brand into a typical Inca pattern.

:Overturn

52 Mindshare

53 The Women's Tennis Association

54 SuperD

52
:Client's Brief
Moving Brands were engaged to define the offer and positioning of Mindshare, as they were going through a global restructure. The strategy needed to support their ambition to regain their market leading position.

:Design Philosophy
The symbol shows two forms coming together to create a new, strong form reflecting Mindshare's partnerships with clients, suppliers and other agencies. This represents the agency's new simplified approach, re-engineering its structure from more than a dozen separate specialist departments to four integrated, collaborative groups. The identity is a "living identity" — coming to life across digital platforms.

53
:Client's Brief
The Women's Tennis Association is the governing body for women's professional tennis. In 2010 this non-profit organization relaunched as a brand independent of its sponsors. The organization needed a logo that would help create independent brand awareness for the WTA.

:Design Philosophy
The firm created a symbol that emphasizes the letters W, T, and A. The new logotype is straightforward and simple while also incorporating references to the sport: the oval shape of the mark alludes to both the imprint a tennis ball leaves on the court and the shape of a racquet, while the yellow circle recalls a tennis ball.

54
:Client's Brief
In order to increase the brand's notoriety on an international level as a cutting-edge technology provider, SuperD entrusted MetaDesign with the development of a new and comprehensive corporate identity, as well as a 3D animated logo to be used in mass marketing communications.

:Design Philosophy
The logotype communicates the power and dynamism of SuperD. The symbol "D" embodies the technology of SuperD: The 3 strokes of the logo come from a ribbon and are overlapped to create a 3D effect. Each color encompasses a quality SuperD represents — blue for technology, purple for passion and grey for a solid foundation.

:Overturn

55 Kallergis Interiors

56 Crown 3 Realty

57 Optima

### 55
**:Client's Brief**

Kallergis Interiors is one of the biggest importers of textiles, leather furniture, panels and roller for residential and commercial use in Greece. The logo and identity represent this large and modern company with emphasis on aesthetics and with respect to its classic, timeless tradition.

**:Design Philosophy**

Kanella Arapoglou focused primarily on typography. The combination of the traditional and the modern feel was achieved by altering a very classic font, Bodoni. The symbol is part of the letter K, and it is used to help the rest of the applications.

### 56
**:Client's Brief**

Crown Three aims to be the most trustworthy, reliable realty firm in the Wichita and surrounding areas. They want their company to exude confidence, friendliness and experience rather than intimidation and obligation.

**:Design Philosophy**

The simplicity of this logo distinguishes Crown Three from their competition by making them appear confident and tasteful. The clean lines and soft curves demonstrate their ability to make a complicated process simple and easy. The mark can be used across many platforms and still deliver its memorable impact.

### 57
**:Client's Brief**

Optima, Belgium's prime financial planning firm, wanted to improve its brand awareness and to underline its unique position as a true specialist with a global vision on all domains: income, property, pension and inheritance.

**:Design Philosophy**

The first element of the new brand identity, the company logo, is constructed of four identical loops, referring to the four domains, that are smoothly linked to one another, as Optima gives their clients comprehensive financial advice.

:Overturn

## ⁵⁸ Tramelan

onlab created the new corporate identity and visual language of the city of Tramelan in Switzerland between 2004 and 2008 and translated the concept into various extensive media and applications.

As an urgent response to 25 years of shrinking and economic regression in Tramelan, an interdisciplinary commission was assigned with the task to examine the identity and development opportunities of Tramelan. onlab was invited to contribute as advisors in the field of communication. After the final report, onlab was commissioned to develop a new visual identity and communication strategy for the village in 2006 and for the years to come.

Key terms of the communication strategy derived from the cultural and historic traits of Tramelan were identified as "Savoir Faire" representing the know-how and craftsmanship of the watchmaker industry and the "Savoir Vivre" representing the authentic lifestyle of the population. These key terms served as conceptual framework for color-coding as well as other formal design features of the visual identity.

:Overturn

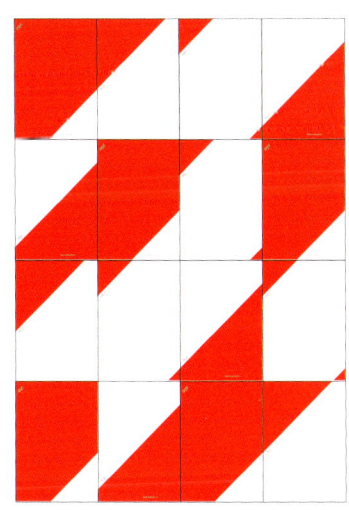  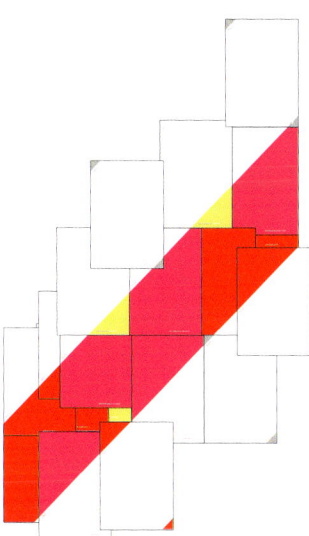

:Overturn

59 STEM Ambassadors

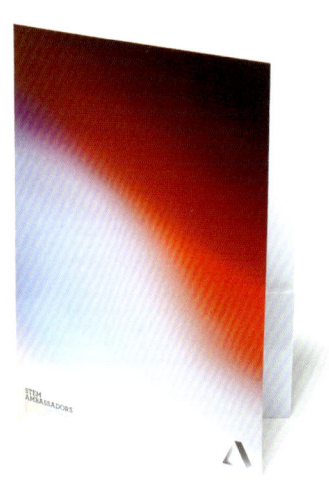

59
:Client's Brief
STEM Ambassadors work within Science, Technology, Engineering and Mathematics (STEM). They visit children in schools to encourage them to engage with STEM subjects and the exciting opportunities these subjects provide. The new identity had to reflect the aims, whilst easy to implement.

:Design Philosophy
Purpose's response was to create an identity around the core thought of illumination and illuminating futures. Central to this is the symbol of a prism, acting as a conduit for transformation and illumination. The visual identity harnesses light and refraction, resulting in a colourful and distinctive identity that works across all touch points.

:Overturn

60 Airtel

61 Swiss Institute of Bioinformatics

62 Barcelona Tribuna

60
:Client's Brief
Evolve the airtel brand in line with the company's global aspirations – in particular transform the dated "corporate feeling" airtel logo into a dynamic consumer brand that belongs to a modern lifestyle sensibility and appeals to a more youthful audience.

:Design Philosophy
The new look and feel design communicates a more contemporary and youthful brand whilst retaining core equities of red and white. The end result is a more modern, confident and dynamic brand identity which works in harmony with the new airtel brand essence of "Enriching Lives".

61
:Client's Brief
SIB required a full revision and restructure of the visual identity, including development of supporting materials

:Design Philosophy
blue-infinity provided a refreshed and modern visual identity whilst retaining the spirit and tradition of the much loved original brand and logo.

62
:Client's Brief
An existing communication platform started a new era; there was a need for updating and showing strength and modernity to new audiences.

:Design Philosophy
Morillas created a subtitle and iconic identity.

:Overturn

63 San Pellegrino Terme

63
:Client's Brief
The territorial branding system of the city of San Pellegrino had to be capable of telling its rich history and its vision of a future currently being built in all its facets: an area attracting elite tourim, where the focus of the experience is both physical and spiritual wellness.

:Design Philosophy
The city's former splendour and current state of the art ambitions has been translated into an ownable brand and communication platform that reinforces the city's identity through all levels of its application, suitable to transfer all properties and virtues of water, which becomes the distinctive element for the entire city identity.

The branding system implied the creation of a corporate typeface, the city signage, spa products branding and package design, digital identity and advertising.

:Overturn

64 Vrionis Music House

65 Bistrot Gourmand

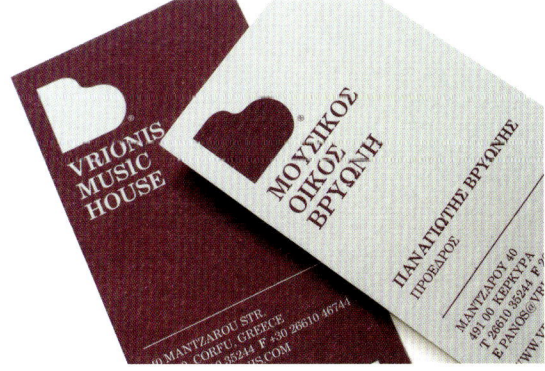

64
:Client's Brief

The aim was to redesign the company's logo, so that it is more aesthetically appealing as well as characteristically distinct. The new logo also had to be prestigious, in order to reflect the company's values and the esteem with which it is held among its target audience.

:Design Philosophy

The logo depicts the outline of a classic piano. The particular instrument was chosen for it constitutes the flagship of any orchestra. Its minimalist, austere shape reflects its value as an instrument while simultaneously, by forming the letter B (the Greek equivalent of the Latin letter "V"), it depicts the initial of the company's name.

65
:Client's Brief

Bistrot Gourmand wanted a warm, and greedy identity, using the two syllables of the name.

:Design Philosophy

Two letters, based on a luxurious font. The "B" and "G" are melt together like chocolate, three colors compose the identity, chocolate brown, custard beige to bind with the gold that represents the precious connotation.

:Overturn

66 The Great Blandini

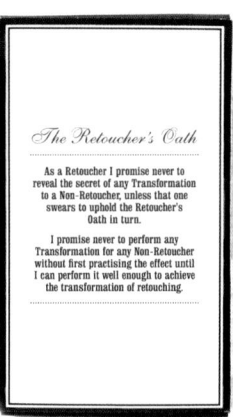

66
:Client's Brief
The objective was to create an identity for the highly skilled retoucher, Steve Bland. He wanted a solution that would stand out from the usual, appeal to the creative industry and reflect his sense of fun and humor.

:Design Philosophy
Steve is a retoucher extraordinaire. Multi-skilled in the mysterious ways of Photoshop. A true Mac wizard. So it was that plain old Steve Bland revealed himself to be The Great Blandini. And with this new identity, an engaging, Victorian-inspired typographic look and feel unfolded, referencing an era when magic was still truly magical.

:Overturn

67 Rebecca Turbow

68 Marta Fernandez

69 DD Design

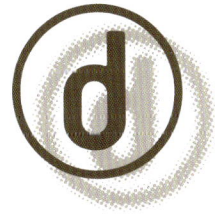 

67
:Client's Brief
Rebecca Turbow wanted to move away from "SAFE" by Rebecca Turbow and simplify it to be just her name. She also wanted the logo to be more fashion forward yet loosely inspired by mod culture.

:Design Philosophy
A playful yet sophisticated mod-inspired logo is always and only shown in silver.

68
:Client's Brief
Marta Fernandez wanted an identity which was fine, feminine, and with style.

:Design Philosophy
To do the best with passion is Negro's design philosophy all the time.

69
:Client's Brief
DD Design wanted to keep a connection to the old logo.

:Design Philosophy
DTM_INC always starts out making a logo in black and white. DTM_INC believes that if it doesn't work in black and white it will never work in color.

:Overturn

70 Cathrine Hammel

71 New Look

72 TESSA

70
:Client's Brief
Cathrine Hammel, a Norwegian fashion designer whose grandfather was a teacher at the Bauhaus and an important role model for her. Her style has later been recognized for her classic signature.

:Design Philosophy
From the rationalist geometric design of the Bauhaus school and the drive to the essentials Designers Journey created a mark with floating geometrical shapes to manifest both the functional component of her research and the archetypal connotation of her collection. The three shapes also function as internal departments: Art, Clothes and Accessories. The font is Gill Sans with capital letters and large spacing.

71
:Client's Brief
New Look occupies over 4 million sq feet of retail space and growing. Their mission is to be at the heart of every fashion conversation. Promoting the New Look brand is key to the organisations success.

:Design Philosophy
SomeOne rebranded New Look ready for the next generation of shoppers. To make it young, fresh and also fashion was the main factor SomeOne considered most.

72
:Client's Brief
TESSA design, produce and sell handbags and women accesories.

:Design Philosophy
TESSA had a distorted and geometric typeface and crown in the logo, which is a very common symbol. A new, modern and more female brand was developed for a new image.

73 Alongkorn

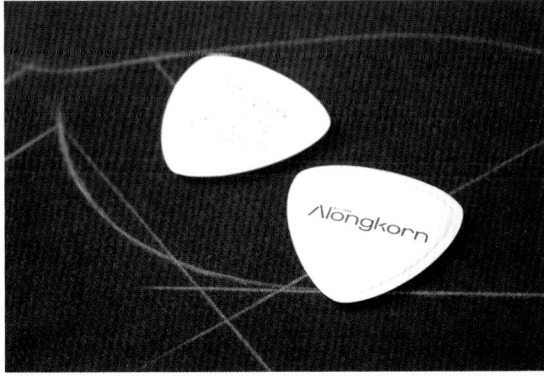
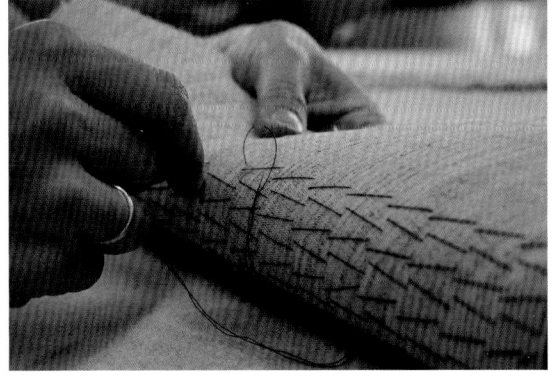

73
:Client's Brief
Alongkorn is a bespoke tailor shop in Bangkok that have been in business since 1958. They wanted to update the brand and make the idea of custom-made appeals more to the younger generation that always buy ready-made suits but at the same time will not loose the classic side and the reputation of high-level craft quality of the brand.

:Design Philosophy
The logo that TNOP came up with based on the hand done pad-stitching that's used as the lining construction of the suit. It represents craft, detail-oriented, classic and sophistication of the brand. The new identity design also reflects craftsmanship and sophistication; especially the business card, it is in a form of the taylor chalk which represents the idea of the custom-made world.

:Overturn

## ⁷⁴ Massimo

**MASSIMO D'ASPI**
*Por León E. Varela*

During the summer of 2010, men's clothing brand, Massimo D' Aspi reached NNSS, with the need of a redesign brand communication. Their main objective was to take Massimo to another level and make it compete with well-known clothing brands. The owner of the firm, Federico D'Aspi, believed that the brand needed a new face, more modern and contemporary without losing what they had built for years.

Massimo was an Italian, born in the town of Ravignano, who at the age of 23 came to Argentina to escape the Second World War. NNSS was surprised to find out while reviewing the pictures, that he was a classic "Italian dandy."

With this information provided by his family, NNSS was able to build the new identity based on two components: the story of his grandfather as an immigrant, the story of a fresh start to conquer their dreams.

And the figure of an authentic Italian Dandy, his characteristic style and card.

NNSS had almost all the elements to create a strong and promising identity, but they needed an icon, an image or object that can sum up the concept. For this reason they include a spice to the story.

NNSS chose the diamond because they represent a valuable object for its beauty and sophistication. Some of what the clothing company is trying to show, is that of European style, elegant and always fashionable.

NNSS build up a simplified logo, which alludes to the octagonal diamond cuts with the M inside. Also it was decided to shorten the name of the brand and leave only the "Massimo" and chose a particular and modern color palette to enhance the idea of "renewal."

In this way the brand presents itself as a hallmark of tradition and identity, which in turn displays an air of renewal and modernization.

The key work focuses on the idea of playing with history, to reinvent it and give free course to imagination.

 INSPIRATION

 FINAL    FINAL

:Overturn

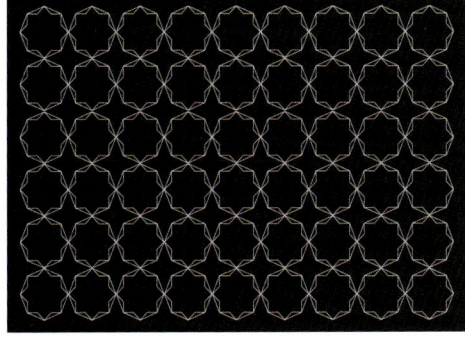

:Overturn

## [75] MK BERGEN

![MK BERGEN logo]

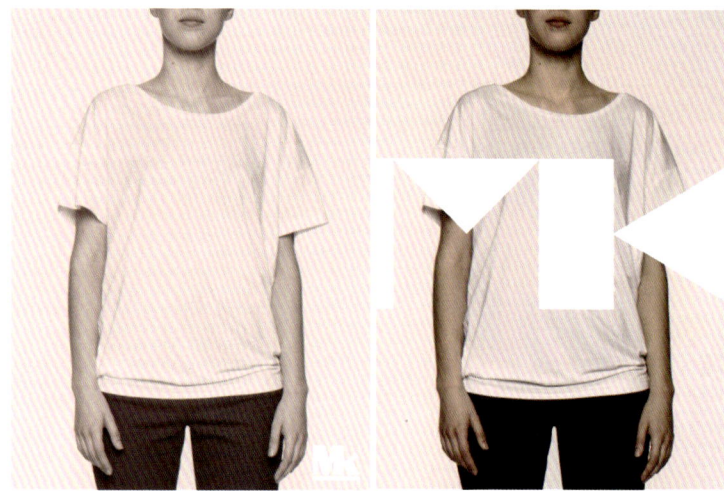

With over 35 years in the communication industry MK is now one of the most experienced studios in the Norwegian market of advertising, design and public relations. As part of a massive redesign of the visual identity in 2009 they asked Grandpeople to provide some fresh opinions on the logo. Their intention was to get Grandpeople involved in the logo development, and then let the in house design team at MK take care of the rest. Grandpeople soon realized that the most efficient approach would be to give themselves full responsibility of every stage of the process.

MK didn't provide Grandpeople with a complete brief, so They had to make one based on their research. Only a few important key factors were presented to them: First, being situated in the periphery of Bergen, far from the capitol of Oslo, MK is working against the odds as a national communication agency with international aspirations. But the company is confident in using this as an advantage. Second, close relations with loyal clients and accounts stretching over a long period of time. Three, the need to reposition MK as a force to be reckoned with nationally, and laying the ground work for an international expansion.

As the new visual identity was to revitalize the image of MK, Grandpeople didn't want to reject the long tradition of trade and commerce embodied within the company (the office building was the oldest one in the oldest trading street in one of the oldest seaports in Norway!). They wanted something fresh and innovative, but not alienating. Something admirable and hopefully surprising. Something clear and concise without being too rigid. They were looking for a contemporary look that wasn't futuristic. They came up with a list of words denoting our ideas: tradition, culture, history, modernism, local identity - international appeal, solid, confident, subtle, sober, serious, craft, authenticity, valuable, responsible, weather proof, scandinavian, nordic, trade, maritime, seaport, wood work, tactile traditional craft - new context, woven extile, wool, stone, concrete, leather, glass, ceramics, porcelain.

:Overturn

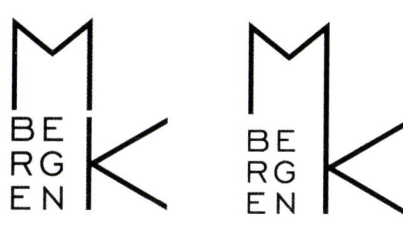

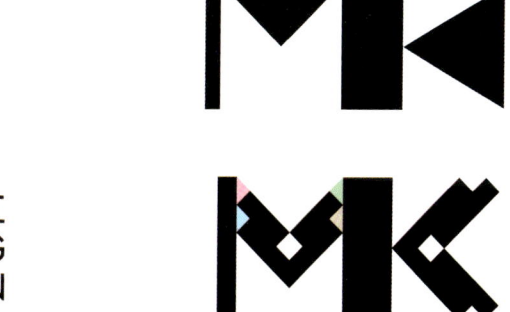

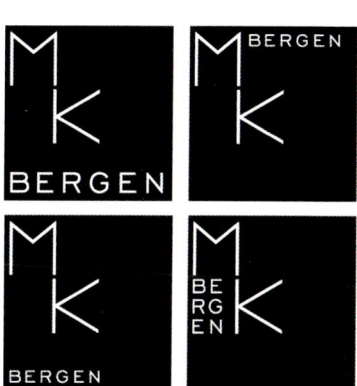

:Overturn

76 Darien Library

77 Brainville

78 Jewish Foundation for Education of Women

76
:Client's Brief
A primary goal was to graphically convey the library's emphasis on "extreme customer service" while cultivating an awareness of its collections, services and programs for all ages. The Yankee culture of the town in combination with the spirit of the library necessitated an identity that would be timeless yet also flexible enough to accommodate continuous advances in technology, service, and media.

:Design Philosophy
The final solution resulted from the simple act of flipping the pages of a book interpreted through a progression of transparent color tints. The logo also refers to a wave, leaves or the wing of a bird, all suggesting movement and ascent.

77
:Client's Brief
The aim was to create a logo and corporate identity, which would give the character of Multimedia City, emerging in the region of Nowy Sacz. Logo had to reflect the consolidation of new technologies and support new businesses.

:Design Philosophy
The Visual identity system is based on the colors of the region — pink and green. The logo is based on the idea of simplicity and minimalism, alludes to the solutions of electronic devices market. Circle as the ideal figure was divided into two symmetrical zones is analogy of the human brain.

78
:Client's Brief
JFEW sought a new logo that would bring emotional significance to its story and contributions to women in the workplace during the 20/21st century, elevate its profile and expand its recognition among academic institutions, nonprofits and JFEW alumni.

:Design Philosophy
The name was reconfigured into a stacked arrangement using Fedra Sans, breaking up the long name and balancing the new symbol that was created to suggest movement and passage, akin to an educational journey that leads to a professional career. The two blues and tints, created through overlaps, express a cool and sophisticated transparency and feminine elegance.

79 Biblionet ID

79
:Client's Brief
Everyone well informed! That is the purpose of Biblionet ID. Biblionet ID has developed digital information portals for more than 100 municipalities in the Netherlands.

:Design Philosophy
In a predominantly large share of the world, the icon "i" means "information". Buro Reng used the icon in the logo design for Biblionet ID and developed the corporate identity, pay-off, website, company brochures, letterhead, product logos, and newsletter.

:Overturn

80 MTV Push

80
The logo adopted the circle as a motif due to the circular "heads" of the Pin Art. The marque inherently being a circle suggests that "Push" is present in every single pin of the pin art and therefore present in every genre of music. This reflects a global outlook and the ability to be intrinsically at the forefront of new music.

Furthermore, this circle that was adopted in the graphic language was intended to strip the element down and serve as a bold, confident addition to the iconic block of the MTV logo.

:Overturn

81 U-Rock

82 Dubbellistig

83 Sabotage

81
:Client's Brief
U-Rock is a high school band contest.

:Design Philosophy
Hula+Hula developed a classic, rock and retro logo for U-Rock.

82
:Client's Brief
The aim was to make the logo more Urban. It's about HipHop.

:Design Philosophy
DTM_INC always starts out making a logo in black and white. DTM_INC believes that if it doesn't work in black and white it will never work in color.

83
:Client's Brief
DJ set needed new versions over the years.

:Design Philosophy
1995 old version was redesigned to become 2000 version with Jesus as icon, used for billposting. 2010 – conceptual version of Sabotage.

:Overturn

84 Fobia

85 DID Records

84
:Client's Brief
Fobia is Mexican Rock band 20th Anniversary logo.

:Design Philosophy
Based on the band's first hand made logo, Hula+Hula added some new elements into the logo to make it more impressive.

85
:Client's Brief
The aim was to create a friendly and easy to read by associating the animal world to the language of techno labels.

:Design Philosophy
Friedrich Santana Lamego simplified the previous logo and made it much easier to be recognized.

86 Tunerfish

86
The friendly fish logo was inspired by the idea that Tunerfish users behave like schools of fish, following each other as they navigate through different television programs. The flexible identity system is designed to represent TV genres ranging from comedy to westerns by having the Tunerfish character dress up in different costumes.

:Overturn

87 Mark Warner

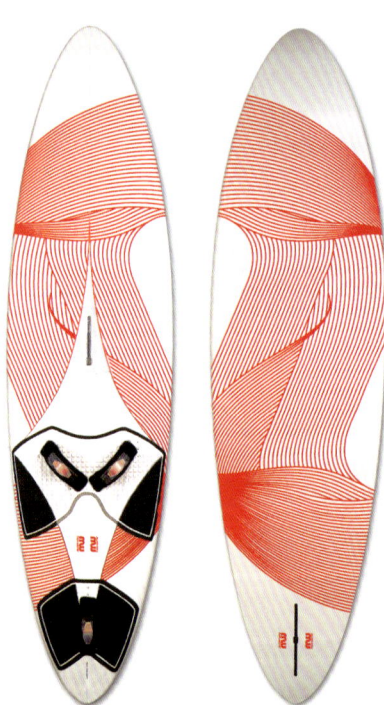

87
:Client's Brief
Mark Warner needed a brand identity which would translate across all branding communications and resort collateral, without traditional "badging". Being useful, cohesive and ensuring everything joins up to the central strategy.

:Design Philosophy
The central strategy SomeOne created — "Feel Free", informed the product, and best described each package, across all communications, from advertising to catalogues. Even on swimsuits. The brand new identity is currently being rolled out Europe-wide.

:Overturn

88 Apollo

89 Vinger

90 Zeeburgia

88
:Client's Brief
The aim was to create a brand identity that is simple, bold and timeless, conveying Apollo as global, confident, modern and relevant.

:Design Philosophy
The design philosophy was simple. Apollo makes tires.

89
:Client's Brief
Vinger asked for anything which is better, more personal and stylish.

:Design Philosophy
Floor Wesseling added the fingerprint, and made it a bit more stylish. Besides, let the brand has their own typeface.

90
:Client's Brief
A modern and more personal (for the team) version needed to instead the very old Zeeburgia logo. Identity of Amsterdam integrated.

:Design Philosophy
The final result is the fusion of classic "Amsterdam school" and graffiti, which is simple to produce as badge developed for Zeeburgia.

:Overturn

91 Golem

92 Beat-Army.org

93 Vinylhund

91
:Client's Brief
Golem found an icon representing the musical universe through a single pictogram.

:Design Philosophy
Friedrich Santana Lamego extracted the element of the previous logo and added the name of the brand into the logo as well.

92
:Client's Brief
Beat-Army.org asked for merging of the collective values of a pictogram, creating a symbol that stays fresh and strong.

:Design Philosophy
Liquify capitals was the main concept for developing new logo of Beat-Army.org.

93
:Client's Brief
A new logo incorporating the image of a dog for a vintage vinyl shop called Vinylhund (vinyl dog), that better illustrated the easygoing atmosphere of the shop as well as the broad range of music styles on sale.

:Design Philosophy
Gytz chose to use a typeface that wouldn't be associated with any sort of music style, moving away from the techno music-inspired lettering, and drew a more jolly and friendly looking dog that better depicted the joy of sniffing out good finds.

:Overturn

94 Sankeys Club

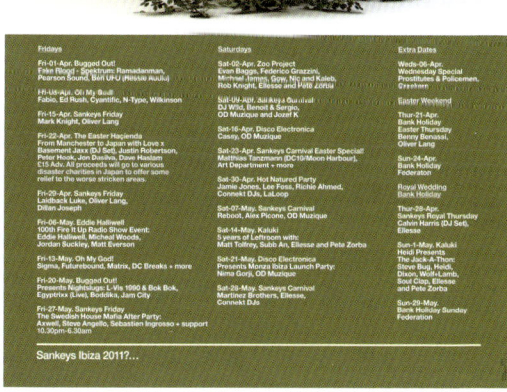

94
:Client's Brief
Sankeys is a world renowned nightclub in Manchester UK. Formally called "Sankeys Soap". They wanted "a new logo doing".

:Design Philosophy
A simple, rememberable device embodies the forward thinking nature of the company and has scope in its applications.

:Overturn

95 Labyrinth Theater Company

96 Saturday Sessions

95
:Client's Brief
Labyrinth Theater Company, or LAB, is known for raw, powerful and moving plays whose stories often involve individuals living at the margins of society.

:Design Philosophy
The new logo conveys the visceral, gritty aspects of their character's lives, while supporting the company's growth during its acclaimed first Broadway show, a brand identity system was developed based on spray painted letterforms akin to graffiti. This uniquely textural symbol has a rough, hand-rendered quality appropriate to their narrative style. The wordmark is given vibrancy and definition from a color palette that combines acid colors on a theatrical, black background.

96
:Client's Brief
Saturday Sessions needed to update the branding for the flagship Saturday night at London's Ministry of Sound to reflect a more edgy and directional music policy.

:Design Philosophy
A new logotype was drawn in 2006 and updated in 2010, based on an 80s-inspired electric script.

:Overturn

97 Tenso

98 La Feliz

99 Club18-30

97
:Client's Brief
Tenso wanted a more solid, more modern and compact logo.
:Design Philosophy
To do the best with passion and be happy is Negro's design philosophy all the time.

98
:Client's Brief
La Feliz wanted a representative logo of its products and its style.
:Design Philosophy
A new typeface was created for the brand.

99
:Client's Brief
The aim was to communicate the excitement of clubbing resort holidays for young people.
:Design Philosophy
The stamp device suggests a sense of belonging and also represents a setting sun, with the message displayed in a bold custom typeface called "Party Machine".

:Overturn

100 ITV Studios

100
:Client's Brief
ITV Productions had changed its name to the more vibrant ITV Studios, and needed a completely new identity. They required the new identity to transform perceptions of what had been ITV Productions, and establish the brand as a high-quality global studio.

:Design Philosophy
The logo aims to reflect the emotions involved in producing and watching quality TV, the peaks and arcs suggest the creativity at the heart of ITV Studios and the colours reference the heritage of ITV and its predecessors. The animation mirrors the creation, spread and amplification of ITV's vision.

:Overturn

1011980 Recordings

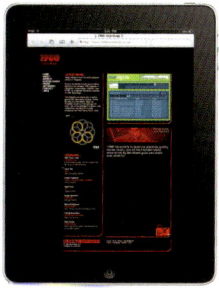 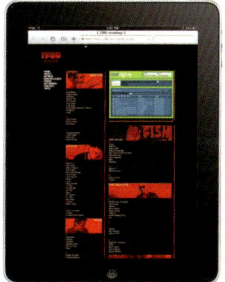 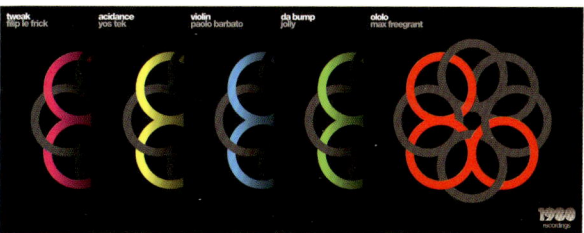

    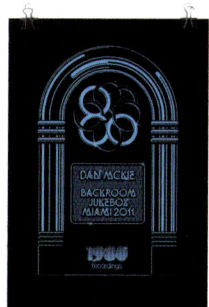

101
:Client's Brief
Electronic music label 1980 recordings required a rebrand to maximise recent high praise by top DJs such as FatboySlim.

:Design Philosophy
After reviewing the existing material it was clear a sharper, more vibrant look was required. This led to the use of clean, bold geometry for the "80" linked rings. For the typography Superfried developed a retro line fade effect creating a subtle connection with the label name.

:Overturn

102 Peter Bailey

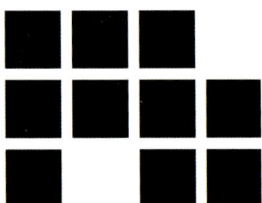

102
:Client's Brief
Peter Bailey approached Bunch for a new logo and an overall facelift.

:Design Philosophy
Bunch created a monogram, which was developed for the use on stationery and promotional materials. Bunch adapted a strong colour palette, which was given to the crew at Peter Bailey's to use as they see fit in order to accompany all photographic material.

103 Noeeko

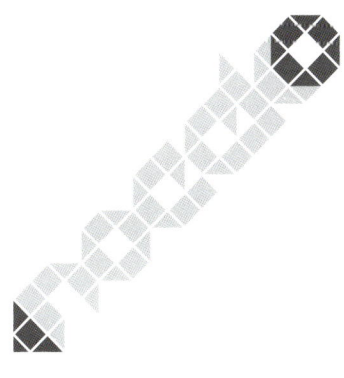 

103
Freelance art director and graphic designer Michal Sycz, whose working name is Noeeko redesigned the logo. It's for his personal use.

:Overturn

104 AWARD

# AWARD.

 AWARD

105 MIB

INTERNATIONAL
SPECIAL
DETECTIVE
FORCE

106 Almo

104
:Client's Brief
AWARD is the benchmark awards individual and school for the advertising industry in Australasia. AWARD came to Interbrand for an identity as creative as the talent it rewards and nurtures, which represented community, participation and involvement of creative individuals.

:Design Philosophy
The centerpiece of the identity is a "living" logo. Each AWARD member and student is represented in the logo by a dot. Controlled by a computer algorithm based on membership numbers, the dots converge, diverge, bounce and swarm. In the printed world, the logo retains its dynamic nature, appearing in a different configuration on every application.

105
:Client's Brief
MIB asked Stas Sipovich to develop a new logo for the MIB International Special Detective Force.

:Design Philosophy
The logo was sharped as a mark on the map, which reflects the meaning of the detective agency, accuracy and professionalism.

106
:Client's Brief
Almo, a leading office supplies company based in the UK, selected Company to re-imagine their brand identity by creating a new logo, stationery, packaging, and product catalogues.

:Design Philosophy
The existing logo, which Almo used for over 60 years was based on a triangular shape. By abstracting the company's initials, A and O, into a triangle and circle Company created a recurring motif that reinforces brand recognition: the products become a background of the visual identity.

:Overturn

107 DJ Dan McKie

107
:Client's Brief
DJ Dan McKie wanted to redesign his personal logo. He required a brand that was distinct whilst maintaining a strong connection to himself.

:Design Philosophy
According to Dan's requirement, a brand that was distinct whilst maintaining a strong connection to himself was designed by Superfried.

:Overturn

108 CDMA

108
:Client's Brief
Fresh, trendy new brand, adopted for a small budgets for production (print, post materials, retail points branding), simple and differentiate from competitors.

:Design Philosophy
Brand formula and claim is simply rational. Color is simple but very powerful and notably — black and white (the main competitors are red and blue). The element of succession is honeycomb — it is used as formative.

:Overturn

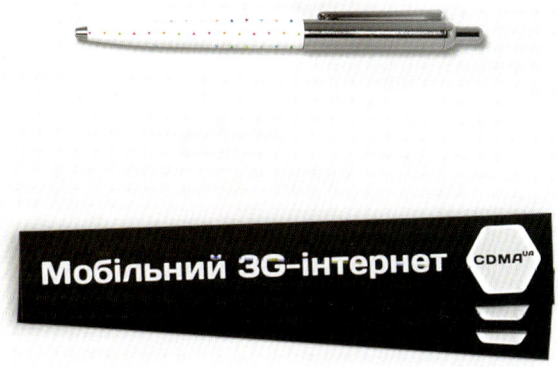

:Overturn

### 109 Calleja

For 85 years, third generation electrical supplier E. Calleja & Sons set the benchmark for the provision of electrical goods in Malta. However, declining market conditions and the sudden death of their Managing Director helped convince the new management team that drastic action would be needed if the brand was to connect with new customers; the way it had in the past.

Bulldog's remit was to help create a new brand positioning, architecture and communication messages that would redefine E. Calleja & Sons as a more contemporary, unified brand.

The project began with research to identify fresh customer insight, key groups and the most powerful benefit for the new brand to own. Following workshops with top management, Bulldog gained a consensus on a brand program. This was documented to help people, both inside and outside the company, understand the intent, spirit and expression of the new brand. Over the years, those who chose E. Calleja & Sons as their preferred electrical supplier did so, more because of interest in a given product, rather than the brand. Calleja hopes to correct this shortcoming through a multi-faceted approach that makes dedication, innovation and accountability in their relationships as important as the products they sell.

:Overturn

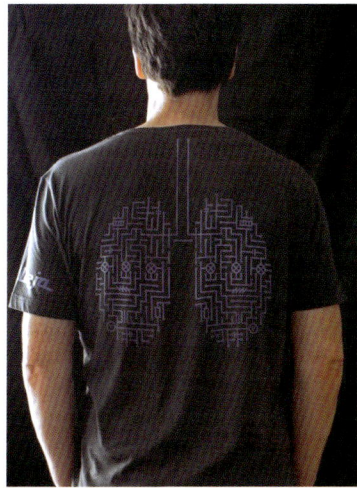
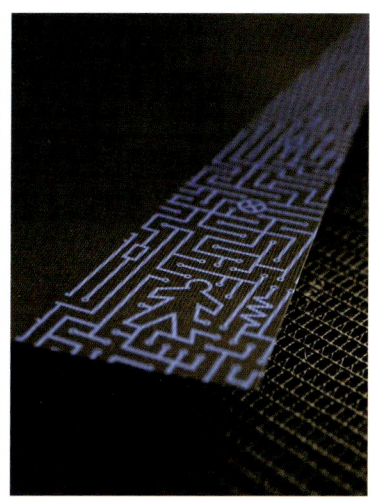

:Overturn

## [110] Aarhus University

Throughout the design programme, the identity integrates a graphic element that is both a storytelling and decorative marker. The element is an abstract alphabet compiled by geometrically simplified letters.

Creating both synergy and consistency across a number of medias throughout the design programme, this abstract alphabet could be viewed as the "fifth element" of the identity. Words and sentences can be written with the alphabet, creating an expressive space for the centers and institutes of the University, making it possible for them to brand themselves while at the same time maintaining a clear, generic visual reference.

The inspiration for the alphabet is drawn from the bricks of the yellow university buildings, or more specifically from the Bauhaus-school, who sought the reduction and simplicity in design and architecture. But also the classic 1934 seal of the University "Solidum petit in profundis" ("Seeking in the depths the solid ground") can be regarded as a source of inspiration. The seal is rooted deeply in the culture and history of the University, and is thus semantically preserved in the new design programme. The logo of the University is written with the abstract alphabet. Along with the seal, the new identity encourages an intelligent and patient quest for broader understanding.

For daily writing purposes, the design programme includes an exclusive and unique typography named "Passata". This creates a consistent and characteristic expression throughout the design program.

:Overturn

111 H.A.N.S  112 CPA

Meet the neighbours

111
:Client's Brief
The aim was to design a new logo and visual style of the HANS construction company, which has to be based on name of the company and has to be readable on all the identity from business card to truck branding.

:Design Philosophy
A logo for the company, which has no permanent fixed value, transforms and changes the shape, staying memorable and easy to read in same time.

112
:Client's Brief
The City Property Association is the authoritative body for property owners and occupiers in the City of London.
Representing and safeguarding the interests of its members and influencing decision makers in local and central government, the organization brings together some of the most influential business leaders in the city.

:Design Philosophy
Purpose created a confident new identity featuring an elegant "key to the City".

:Overturn

113 Bern

114 NBC Universal

115 Chase Manhattan Bank

113
:Client's Brief
Bern asked for a logo to honour the city, Bern, the capital of Switzerland.

:Design Philosophy
The bear is the original heraldic animal of Bern, but what really shapes the city is the Aare River. (This logo was part of the project CitID and was never implemented.)

114
:Client's Brief
The merger with Comcast demanded a revisit of NBC universal logotype. The media entertainment giant needed something more relevant to its new growth and vision.

:Design Philosophy
Embrace the historical typographic details of the NBC and Universal logotypes and make something unique and contemporary. The new logotype needed to be comfortable in the presence of many brands across cable, broadcast, digital, parks & resorts and film industries.

115
Two historic banks, the Chase National Bank and the Bank of the Manhattan Company, merged in 1955 to form the Chase Manhattan Bank. The new firm embarked on constructing what was then a radical aluminum-and-glass, 60-story skyscraper in New York's financial district.

To better reflect the new bank's scope and power, in 1960 Chermayeff & Geismar designed an octagonal-shaped symbol to boldly identify the many retail outlets and considerable advertising exposure for what had become the nation's largest bank. At the time, few American corporations used abstract symbols for their identification. Radical for its time, the Chase symbol has survived a number of subsequent mergers and has become one of the world's most recognizable trademarks.

116 Library of Congress

117 SETI Institute

118 National Library of Ireland

---

116
:Client's Brief
In 2006, the Library of Congress completed a year-long study to establish an updated brand positioning and a coordinated messaging policy. Chermayeff & Geismar was then hired to create a new graphic identity for the Library and to develop a comprehensive new identity system for the Library's many divisions and associated entities.

:Design Philosophy
The centerpiece of the new identity system is a symbol that distills and joins the essence of a book and the American flag to represent the national library.

117
:Client's Brief
Communicate the SETI Institute's dual mission: 1) Astrobiology research into the origin of life on earth and the search for any forms of life elsewhere in the solar system — even single cell organisms, and 2) Search for signs of sentient life — no longer reliant only on radio telescopes — but optical telescopes as well.

:Design Philosophy
The logo's dual meaning can be interpreted as cell division or other broad themes in the pursuit of discoveries in astrobiology, as well as the search for signs of intelligent life in the vast universe of stars and optical or radio "noise".

118
:Client's Brief
The new logo was designed as part of an overall identity programme. The function of the identity is to bring an overarching consistency to the points of engagement between the Library and its many audiences which include the general public. To increase awareness and visibility of the National Library in general.

:Design Philosophy
The National Library of Ireland icon is a simple graphic representation of the letters N, L and I, the N coming from the curves of the arches and windows, synonymous with the architecture of the Library building itself and the period it was built and the L and I from the columns which are commonly found alongside the arches.

:Overturn

119 Amsterdam Student Festival

120 Forward Step

121 MMCD

119
:Client's Brief
Amsterdam Student Festival is an annual event where students can put their artistic skills on display. The organization has to work hard each year to gather all the needed funds for the event. They needed a logo that was more in touch with the financial world than their current one.

:Design Philosophy
Calango took the opportunity to separate the identities of the festival and it's organization. This way the organization could take a more corporate feel, while the festival campaign could keep its arty appearance.

120
:Client's Brief
The aim was to redesign the current brand identity of "Forward Step" to convey a message of hope and optimism as opposed to despair.

:Design Philosophy
The redesigning aimed to use blocks as a dynamic element to drive the concept of hope, success and achievement.

121
:Client's Brief
MMCD's requirement was to redesign but not to be all new, and to keep a visually link to the old logo.

:Design Philosophy
The company's main focus on scientific multimedia is pictured by the use of a world map while the design plays with a front (pixeled) and back version (sharp) of the logo on the printed media.

:Overturn

122 Interclick

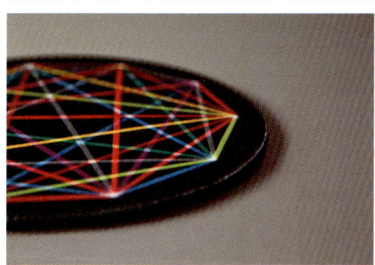

122
:Client's Brief
Stand out from within the top 25 ad networks. Build a recognizable, memorable brand experience. Design a clear and unified system that's confident, smart, and able to lead the industry with proprietary tech solutions. Less negative. More positive.

:Design Philosophy
The logo holds the essential branding components, serves as the launch pad for growing the system and expanding it into sub-brands and parallel businesses. The matrix sphere represents how Interclick connects consumers with other consumers, with publishers and with other brands. A dynamic system of colors and lines combined to create a memorable, unique and engaging experience of the brand.

:Overturn

123 Design Wars

123
:Client's Brief
The main idea was to create the sign based on pencil and drop of paint.

:Design Philosophy
Design Wars' logo has an image of pencil and paint drop which represent design. If observed closely one can see the eye which represents Death Star from Star Wars.

:Overturn

124 My Eskimo Friend

124
MEF is a creative communications agency. They have assembled a full spectrum of creative skillsets that span the globe. MEF methodology is to harvest an elite team of talents from various creative fields with synergy that flows across international boundaries. TomTor Studio helped them to restyle their logo and the whole image of the brand.

:Overturn

125 Basement Media

125
TomTor Studio was commissioned to redesign Basement Identity System's marketing campaign. BM is a full-service creative marketing design firm located at the nucleus of entertainment, art, and progressive modern design that caters to global lifestyle consumers and brands in the United States and Japan. Their advertising, strategic planning, print design, corporate branding, relationship marketing, event sponsorships, interactive websites, digital marketing, visual effects, post production, media planning / buying, public relations, and promotions, range from full scale productions of broadcast commercials to music videos, which integrate the techniques of visual Feng Shui.

:Overturn

:Overturn

126 Creative Memories

127 New French Bakery

128 Formul'habitat

126
:Client's Brief
Creative Memories, the world's leading scrapbook company, producing products that are fun and fresh. Yet the Creative Memories logo hadn't been updated in twenty years. And they needed a new logo to reflect these attributes, while holding onto the company's heritage and 20-year history.

:Design Philosophy
The new logo is fun and friendly, as well as highly recognizable thanks to a design that contains varied type, representing the different stories of scrap bookers. The color blue is a tribute to Creative Memories' heritage, and an icon that is a stylized version of a camera's aperture where the scrap booking process begins.

127
:Client's Brief
The design objective was to disrupt the boring brown of grocery bakeries and to celebrate the simple joys of fresh baked bread. The classic fleur-de-lis, the French symbol of artisan quality, was transformed into a modern background pattern, playing contrast to a bold new brand language and identity.

:Design Philosophy
A design system is meant to project a fresh mix of French artistry and everyday revelry in a true celebration of the delights of fresh beaked, warm bread. Design elements included: brand identity, packaging program, point of sale materials, collateral, website design, promotional pieces and stationery system.

128
:Client's Brief
The aim was to redesign the historical identity while keeping the abbreviations "FH" for the house construction company called "Formul'habitat".

:Design Philosophy
A more sophisticated logotype while illustrating a house ark with the letters "FH" was designed.

:Overturn

129 Zefiro

130 LM Wind Power

129
:Client's Brief
Zefiro needed to build a new brand identity able to reflect and clearly communicate their property to their audience, without compromising the perception of the unique common root of the two branches.

:Design Philosophy
The logotype was flipped into two different shapes: a circle and a square. The circle represents the idea of protection, collaborativism, growth, reinforced by the chosen color: a nice, relaxing blue. The square communicating solidity, stability, concreteness, is divided into two rectangles — and from the orange color of the bricks the link to another image: the track fields. Fago typeface was used for the brand.

130
:Client's Brief
Make® was asked to take on the lead agency role for the rebranding – providing the core concept and liaising with other agencies to ensure a smooth implementation around the world.

:Design Philosophy
The new identity demonstrates that LM Wind Power is a company with a strong corporate profile that can meet the global needs of its current and future customers.

:Overturn

131 Finance & Credit

132 Microspray

131
:Client's Brief
Finance & Credit resorted to rebranding.

:Design Philosophy
Push button was developed as the logo and the consistent form of the whole identity.

132
:Client's Brief
Microspray is an Italian industrial company which manufactures spray valves for pharmaceutical products.

:Design Philosophy
NNSS added the human character to the brand by working on a dual concept: finished product and consumer, giving the company's image more warmth.

133 Binc

134 Bike Ribbon

135 Endace

133
:Client's Brief
Binc is an international player in luxury interior design and asked Calango to redesign the logo in a way that it could be used for the different activities of the fast expanding interior design company.

:Design Philosophy
Calango took the luxurious and contemporary feel of the brand as a startingpoint and made a custom typeface. It was used to create a monogram and separate logo for the brands' subdivisions with the same formula.

134
:Client's Brief
Bike Ribbon is a leading racing and mountain bike accessories brand. The project involves restyling the entire corporate identity, and it started with the new logo. The client's requirement was to redesign his identity in order to convey an idea of the brand more up-to-date.

:Design Philosophy
The spiral – a key, historical element for the company – has been redesigned. The aim was for a flexible, memorable look. Alongside this contemporary, dynamic symbol, jekyll & hyde placed simple, very clear lettering. Finally, for the corporate colour they chose a deeper shade of the orange hue that has always identified the company.

135
:Client's Brief
Endace, one of New Zealand's technology exporting success stories and a world leader in network monitoring, asked us to help them create a more professional and visible brand that stripped away the technical complexity of what they do and clearly communicated their point of difference to their customers.

:Design Philosophy
As part of the brand refresh Everything Design developed a new logotype that has a clear visual reference to the human eye — symbolising the company's commitment to giving client organisations the "power to see all".

:Overturn

136 Promenade

# Promenade

136
:Client's Brief
As sale was down and the package design was dated, Promenade decided to refresh the identity of the product and the whole package design. The goal was to maintain the charm of the French clichés but in a more contemporary key to be able to attract a younger segment of Promenade drinkers but not loosing the faithful followers.

:Design Philosophy
Designers Journey developed a set of key values: A walk through France. Souvenir de Paris. Romance, elegance and charm. They worked with more detailed hand drawn elements compared to the existing artwork.

137 Heimen

138 Twist & Tango

---

137
:Client's Brief

Heimen was founded in 1922 and is the oldest existing shop and cultural archive of original Norwegian patterns and textiles used for national costumes. The cultural house also includes Hotel Bondeheimen which is the resident café that offers a traditional Norwegian cuisine with ingredients from small local suppliers around the country.

:Design Philosophy

The job was to do a deep analysis of the true values of the company to make sure this part of national history was blending with the goal of moving into the future and to still be an attractive institution for the new generation to come.

138
:Client's Brief

Twist & Tango wanted to update the logo to the new, younger look and feel of the brand.

:Design Philosophy

The new logo was developed to be classic, timeless but still "new".

:Overturn

139 360 Architecture

139
:Client's Brief
Two companies were merged to become one brand. Hence, a new logo and whole identity are needed for this brand new company.

:Design Philosophy
Design Ranch creates an image that encompasses the firm's full spectrum of offerings, and focuses on its strength of sports architecture.

:Overturn

140 Spackman Mossop and Michaels

141 Dag Van De Architectuur Groningen

140
:Client's Brief
Spackman Mossop and Michaels asked Erik Kiesewetter to develop a new identity.

:Design Philosophy
Apply an international style that is both clean and concise for use in both offices in the US and Australia.

141
:Client's Brief
The Day of Architecture (Dag Van De Architectuur Groningen) is a major annual European event, since 1986. The aim was to raise awareness of architecture in the widest possible audience.

:Design Philosophy
Letters become architecture. Buro Reng developed a dynamic logo that appears to be 3D. There are several versions of the logo, wide and narrow. For the Day of Architecture in Groningen Buro Reng designed the corporate identity, a logo animation, website and poster-brochure.

:Overturn

## 142 Melbourne Convention Exhibition Centre

**What does your client hope to achieve through redesigning the logo?**

The client expectations were: The strategic creation of a distinctive identity in the crowded Convention and Tourism sector — internationally and locally; symbolise the brand idea of "Melbourne's Meeting Place" which underpins the MCEC story; own a graphic icon (the letter "M") which speaks to all audiences and will become a valuable communication asset.

**What did you consider most when redesigning the logo?**

We considered what the brand mark was required to represent — Melbourne's leading edge Convention and Exhibition centre; where it was to be used-throughout all Communications and environmental implementation; and how it could add value to MCEC as a business when it talks to local and global audiences. Importantly, the MCEC brand mark application extended across a range of materials, so its efficient reproduction was essential.

**Compared to the previous logo, the new logo is much younger and more vigorous. It seems to be the function of the color you employed in the new logo. What's the concept of using these colors?**

Our aim was to reflect the energy of the Convention and Exhibition Centre as a dynamic "people place" and to ensure that the brand mark design could be integrated into the built form. The new MCEC brand mark is an active design which contains the visual wit of an optical illusion as the graphic "M" can be viewed as both flat and as a three dimensional shape. It was important for us, that the new MCEC benchmark created an engaging, emotional connection with audiences.

The colours were chosen to be optimistic and create a unique balance between the warm hues of the colour spectrum. The orange is used throughout the interior design and the pink accent acts as a beacon of colour intensity. Owning a colour composition aids recognition and distinction.

**Apparently the logo was developed from character "M", but why did you shape the "M" this way?**

The 'M' letterform symbolises the City of Melbourne. It also provides the basis of the design story that is about a sense of style (conventions and exhibitions) and a sense of place (an iconic architect designed building).

**From your professional point of view, are there any durable logos? Or the logos need to meet with time changes?**

In the brand world, all brand imagery must remain relevant to the story that a business wants to share with its marketplace. As this brand story evolves, so must the brands communication and visual language. A well considered identity can be the constant lighthouse for an organisation's brand messaging. As marketing communication changes to suit marketplace strategies, the identity remains a reminder of what the organisation stands for. However, even the most robust identity may need adjustment to ensure that it does not look dated. This may be through refinement of shape, colour or typography. In the case of the MCEC, a completely new brand story was required. The original design was based upon an architectural emphasis. When the new Convention and Exhibition building was created, there was a need for an identity with a story, that would become a valuable marketing asset, identifying the MCEC in a way that could be understood, admired and add distinction across all applications.

:Overturn

143 CooperVision

144 DermaMed Solutions

143
:Client's Brief
The new brand refresh expresses the unique approach and perspective CooperVision brings to the business of contact lenses and celebrates the optimism and enhanced lifestyle that contact lenses provide.

:Design Philosophy
Visually represented through a beautiful array of watercolors, the new design offers an original and unexpected take on the concept of moisture.

144
:Client's Brief
The aim was to keep the positive energy of the existing icon but make it more 2011.

:Design Philosophy
To try to keep the logo simple was the main concept throughout the whole redesigning process.

:Overturn

145 The Y

146 Alhurra

### 145
**:Client's Brief**

The Y is now poised to more powerfully articulate how it nurtures the potential of youth, improves health and fosters a sense of social responsibility.

**:Design Philosophy**

Around the adoption of a nickname for the organization — a recognition of what had already become its facto name: the Y, Siegel+Gale crafted an engaging visual system, incorporating a range of bright color combinations that mirrors the Y's diversity of programs and audiences.

### 146
**:Client's Brief**

Alhurra wanted to have new on-air television graphics and a web presence that would give the network a strong brand image, signal a shift in programming toward more news-oriented content and appeal to a younger demographic.

**:Design Philosophy**

The logo, three flowing colored ribbons that coalesce to form a bird in flight, speaks to the network's goal to broaden its viewers' perspectives. The ribbons evoke banners, flags and celebration, while the bird symbolizes superiority, light, freedom and aspiration, all attributes consistent with a network dedicated to accurate, balanced and comprehensive news.

:Overturn

147 Zhengwei Group

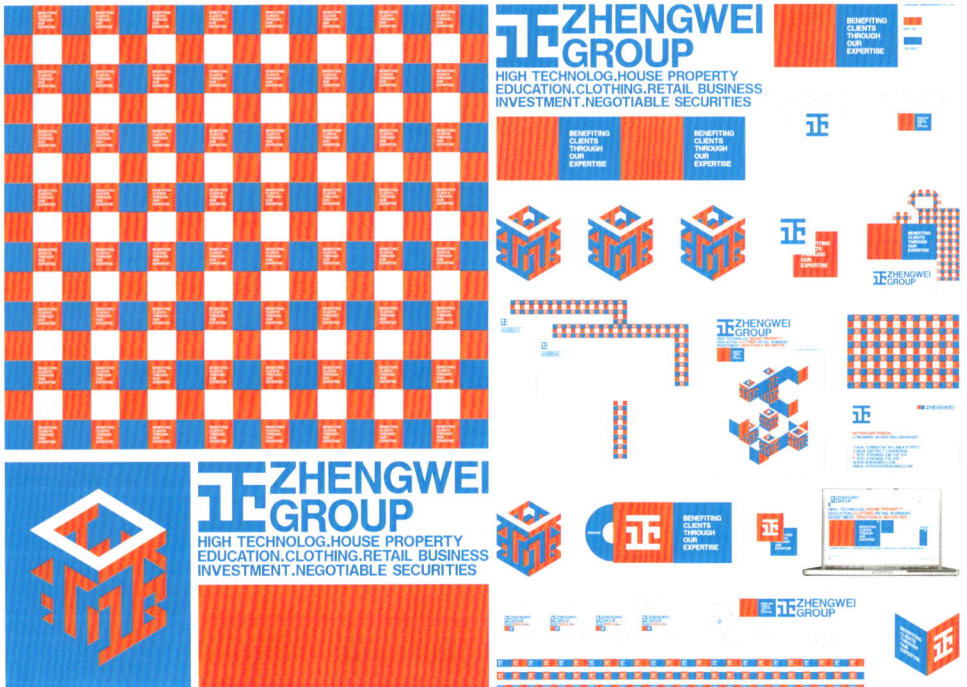

147
:Client's Brief
Zhengwei Group is a multi-industry company which is rapidly developing and almost reaching the peek at present. For elevating company's cohesion and marketability, they needed a new visual identity.

:Design Philosophy
Resonance designed a character "正" having slogan "BENEFITING CLIENTS THROUGH OUR EXPERTISE" cooperated with as two squares. The red and yellow squares are coherent forming different combination. As basic promotional elements, they have simple regulation as well as various formations in different media.

:Overturn

148 Xingu Commercial 06 Exhibition

149 Guangke Fishery

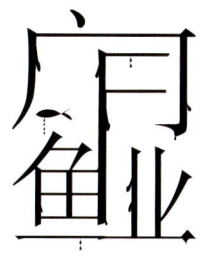

150 Shitang Management

### 148
:Client's Brief
Xingu Commercial 06 Exhibition is a commercial exhibition displaying cultural products. How to make the characteristic of the exhibition prominent in the strong commercial atmosphere became the difficulty that the design project encountered.

:Design Philosophy
Resonance directly used "06 展" as the simple symbol of the logo. "06展" here is much like a graphical epitome of three-dimensional space enveloped by red.

### 149
:Client's Brief
Guangke Fishery is a Dalian Famous brand which manufactures marine products.

:Design Philosophy
Chinese characters were applied in the new logo. The droplet on the characters manifests the freshness of the marine products of the brand.

### 150
:Client's Brief
Shitang Management has invested in twelve big fields, especially IC card, a rational and general form. This particularity determined that the identity shall be out of the ordinary.

:Design Philosophy
Character "世" was created within twelve small grids in a square emphasizing the original concept of the brand. Golden is daringly used as the color of the identity which can highlight the theme.

:Overturn

151 Kaplan Thaler Group

152 Minstrel

153 Bernardino

---

**151**
**:Client's Brief**
The Kaplan Thaler Group is a well-known advertising agency in New York City. C&G Partners was asked to rebrand the agency.

**:Design Philosophy**
C&G Partners decided to do away with the literal and overused "idea" lightbulb image, but to keep it as a hand-drawn and ever-changing pet which pops up on stationery, on the web, and in animation. In the logo, the lightbulb idea is expressed with a central, yellow, and sometimes glowing letter "A." C&G Partners convinced the agency to really own the color yellow and to make it a part of their identity.

**152**
**:Client's Brief**
Minstrel goes from artist to being a label, new logo needed, more now – modern.

**:Design Philosophy**
Modern version and was added the production part.

**153**
**:Client's Brief**
To design a more modern logo able to communicate stability, protection, concreteness and conomic value. The main goal was to gain condence from potential local clients by making a global facelift of San Bernardino's visual identity built around a new, solid, bold, strong logo.

**:Design Philosophy**
A strong distinctive sign was needed so Blumagenta designed an emblem inspired by the beehive's internal structure hexagonal cells, shaped it into a house-like icon with the stylized "SB" initials positioned inside. Then Blumagenta came to the logotype design customizing the clean, elegant, modern, Avenir typeface.

:Overturn

154 Virtuele Straat

155 HakaGroup

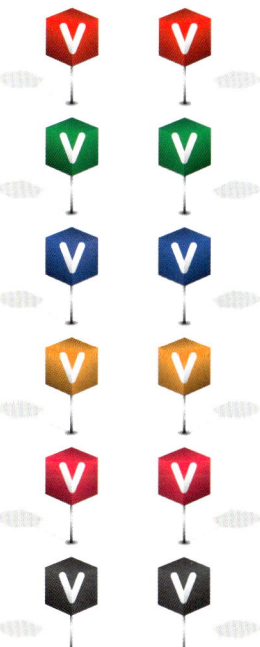

154
:Client's Brief
Old version is very attractive but less communicative.

:Design Philosophy
The new version was better to use, functional for the purpose; the website and landmarking.

155
Company engaged in event-organization and entertainment for young people. Corporate image showing the conceptual essence of the company. Getting away from the routine. Escaping from boredom. It is very interesting how these values can be shown through the traffic sign of "men working".

:Overturn

156 First Citizens Bank

157 New York State Restaurant Association

158 LSI

156
:Client's Brief
The strategic repositioning and image revitalization coincide with the Group's emergence as the top internationally rated Bank in Trinidad and Tobago and marks the expansion of the Group's services and capabilities.

:Design Philosophy
Multiple colors in the identity were inspired by the vibrant multicultural environment in which First Citizens operates, as well as the diversity within the global markets. The color green is still predominant, to build on the existing equity that the company has built throughout its history in the market. The modern First Citizens logotype is friendly and communicates the Group's flexibility and commitment to customers.

157
:Client's Brief
Responding to a decline in membership, the New York State Restaurant Association sought to modernize its image and evolve its messaging to better emphasize the value it provides to its members.

:Design Philosophy
A new logo was developed based on a circular intersection of essential dining tools — fork, knife, spoon, chopsticks — intended to convey not merely the business sector but that the strength of the organization lies in the exchange of information and expertise between its members. A yellow-to-green gradient color palette gives the design warmth and freshness, valuable assets to the hospitality trade.

158
:Client's Brief
LSI Logic and Agere merged to form the new LSI, a leader in silicon-to-systems solutions for storage, networking and consumer markets. Liquid was asked to develop not just a new logo — but a new comprehensive brand identity system.

:Design Philosophy
Innovation is at the heart of LSI. Liquid created a sophisticated logotype that shows how LSI confidently stand behind their ideas; the spark, the symbol of the enduring and inspiring spirit of innovation.

:Overturn

159 Pula is More

159
:Client's Brief
Pula Tourist Board commissioned a rebranding project to improve the competitiveness of City of Pula as a tourist destination.

:Design Philosophy
A modular visual communication system which visually depicts a combination of Pula's qualities was created.

:Diversity

### 01 Waterstone's

The book market is changing, with online competitors and supermarkets grabbing market share, and the Kindle and iPad transforming the way we read. Waterstone's is the UK's national book retailer with over 300 stores. But it was starting to feel tired, old and uninspiring. The challenge was to re-establish Waterstone's as the best place for everything new and exciting and brilliant about books.

venturethree worked with Waterstone's to create a new vision for the brand, powerful enough to reignite the booksellers' passion, to inspire a new identity and to reinvent the stores. From staid and stuffy, to the most exciting destinations on the High Street.

A love of books was put back at the heart of the brand, with a generous new invitation to "feel every word". venturethree's approach was to create a modern cultural icon. The W symbol was retained but took on a contemporary new form. It was then rendered in a myriad of different ways to reflect different genres, characters and stories. Expressing the richness and excitement of the Waterstone's offer.

The shops needed to change dramatically, without a refit. So venturethree created a new graphic system and tone of voice to shake them up through everything from wall vinyls to point of sale materials and campaigns.

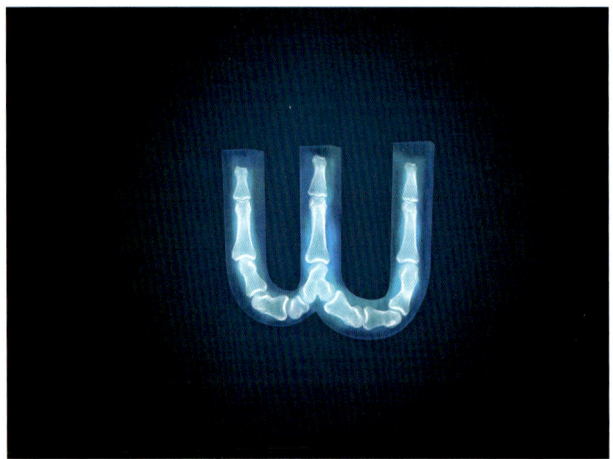

:Diversity

:Diversity

## 02 City of Melbourne

**Why did City of Melbourne want to redesign the logo? What did City of Melbourne require on the redesign?**

City of Melbourne is a dynamic, progressive city, internationally recognized for its diversity, innovation, sustainability, and livability. City of Melbourne council supports the city's world-class offerings, represents it nationally and internationally, and ensures it remains a preeminent Australian center for culture, arts, dining, entertainment, education, and shopping. Since implementing its previous identity 15 years ago, City of Melbourne has experienced significant change. As a result, the council had accumulated a range of isolated logos for various services, which had become increasingly difficult and costly to manage. The fragmentation of City of Melbourne's identity meant equity was driven away from the core brand, and the council realized that it needed a long-term solution.

City of Melbourne asked us to develop a cohesive brand strategy and new identity system. The challenge was to reflect City of Melbourne's cool sophistication on the world stage, capture the passion of its people, and provide the city with a unified, flexible, and future-focused image. The new identity needed to overcome political complexities, improve the cost-effectiveness of managing the brand, and unite the disparate range of entities (including the council, City of Melbourne's destination brand, and an ever-growing portfolio of different initiatives, programs, services, events, and activities).

**How does the new logo present City of Melbourne?**

This new identity is the physical manifestation of the organization's deepest commitment to the city's values. That's an internal drive and the culture can rally around the principles that went into the design. But it was also built with the public firmly in mind: residents, visitors, local and national government, the media, suppliers etc.

We built the branding program on the results of a thorough audit of City of Melbourne's various identities and its long-term sustainability and strategic plans. The audit assessed public opinion and interviewed stakeholders who included local government officials, business owners, and community representatives. The work drew out where the organization is currently and where it is going in the future.

**Compared to the old logo, the new logo advances with the times, what progress did the new logo make?**

For an organization like City of Melbourne, the vast array of offerings requires a multitude of communications and applications. The requirement was for an identity system that could work at varying scales across all kinds of media. It had to communicate the brand idea instantly and establish recognition of author, whilst conveying the various needs and specific requirements of each service, initiative or event. The new identity would eventually live across the full gamut of applications – signage, literature, corporate communications, digital media, advertising, uniforms, vehicles, events, banners, instillations, environments, and appear equally powerful whether on a street banner or the rubbish bins for residents.

The identity system embraces the idea of change and adaptation to circumstances and surroundings, especially with the increasingly varied arena of media usage. There is a need to maintain consistency and clarity of voice from City of Melbourne, but we were conscious of the fact that to get the best results in the rollout of these materials we needed to create a system that people wanted to get involved in. The over-arching principles are there to be followed, but more than this, they are there to be a source of inspiration for the in-house teams and the variety of creative partners in the years to come.

:Diversity

:Diversity

**The design of the new logo is totally different from the old one. Do you think it took risk to do the changeover? If so, what risk was it?**

With an ever-increasing homogeneity and visual clutter vying for our attention, the key is to differentiate. Standing out from the crowd is nothing new to our ears, yet is a lot harder than you would imagine. For most companies and organizations, to radically differentiate is to do what nobody else is doing. The uncertainty of following this path is what prevents the majority from actioning such a move. There will always be barriers to real change. By dismantling uncertainty for our clients we can break the paradigm of over-cautiousness, and really push things forward. "New" is different, it's difficult to grasp and it's uncomfortable.

The risk with any new identity is a lack of understanding. All too often progressive branding programmes that aren't embedded in organisational strategy, or that don't have buy-in at the highest level, struggle to eventuate as anything but a compromised identity. Branding, now more than ever, is about owning the idea, putting it at the heart of the organisation, and enabling it to spread across all touch-points and channels, no matter how much the media landscape changes.

**Bold "M" is the outline of the logo and it's undiversified, why was the bold "M" designed? And what symbolic meaning does it have?**

Each person's Melbourne is different, made up of hundreds of combinations of services and experiences, but they work together to make up Melbourne as a whole. City of Melbourne had to be everything to everybody. It needed to be relevant to and reflective of all demographics, all ages, all interests. It had to be the council organization that runs everything from the Christmas and New year festivities, Spring fashion week, festivals and services whilst simultaneously taking the responsibility for urban planning, sustainability of the city, utilities, community development and on top of this hand out parking tickets. Quite the tall order.

At the heart of the new design, the bold "M" presents a full expression of the identity system – immediately recognizable and as multifaceted as the city itself: creative, cultural, sustainable. A celebration of diversity and personal interpretation that is both future-proof and iconic. The final form of the identity was developed after a thorough development stage where every type of "M" form was explored. In the end, the geometry of the M provided not only a structure underlying the identity, just like the city itself, but also a unique canvas that enabled hundreds of iterations.

:Diversity

**Within the bold "M", the color and the pattern is various. What is it aim for?**

If colour is the most immediate form of non-verbal communication, then it made sense that it should play a key role in creating an instantly recognizable and differentiated Identity. With City of Melbourne, the challenge was to reflect the many different aspects of the organization, from authoritative, restrained and serious, through to a vibrant, visionary and passionate.

Melbourne is known to be a highly creative city. With it's inspiring architecture, public art and sculpture and the diverse range of cultural events that are held within the city, it seemed highly appropriate to bring this intrinsic diversity and enriched living to life through a full spectrum of colours. It not only demonstrates the life within the organization, but the energy and inspiration that is inherent in this progressive city of culture.

**What influence and benefit can the new logo system bring about for City of Melbourne?**

The frequency of discussion in the public about design and branding has spread beyond the industry magazines and into public debate. This is especially true when the project is firmly in the public eyes, such as a new consumer service, a national or international event. The branding of cities and countries can't help but elicit a multitude of responses and emotions through a sense of pride and ownership of the people that ultimately need to be engaged.

The City of Melbourne Identity has generated an enormous amount of opinion and articles by everyone from industry leaders, students and even cab drivers. The range of media exposure and commentary has spanned a plethora of media, from the traditional media of Newspapers, Television, and word of mouth through to a multitude of social media platforms — Twitter, Facebook, YouTube, Behance, Blogs, and Cataloging sites. The speed at which the global commentary and debate has spread is a positive — people are engaged (even if at times, it is critical engagement). The indifference that previously existed has evolved into healthy debate that can only aid in the development of how we choose to represent cultures and cities through visual identities.

:Diversity

## ⁰³ OCAD University

**What is your clients's requirement on the redesign?**

The institution had been given degree-granting status and needed a name change. It was no longer "Ontario College of Art and Design" as the old identity had it, but instead OCAD University.

**Different elements can be put into the biggest square in the new logo, namely, the new logo can be endowed with various elements. How do you come up with this idea? What do you want to convey through this logo?**

The elements are students' artworks. Every year the graduates who win a Medal of Honour will be able to contribute to the "window" and create new logos. There will be a fleet of logos for use that year and the next year, when new students graduate, a new group will be able to create the coming year's logos. We wanted the logo to expose the talent and work of the students and riffed off the windows of the Will Alsop building and the idea of being able to look inside.

**Generally the logos of schools or academies are quite stiff. But the logo of OCAD is apparently not of that kind. But new things are not easy to be accepted by the public. Were you under any pressure when developing this logo? And what was that?**

We engaged in a very inclusive and extensive research process, and that helped us understand the kind of institution we were working with: culturally rich, conceptually and aesthetically engaged and risk-takers from the beginning 135 years ago. We articulated that challenge verbally and then worked very hard to meet it. We understood the importance of this institution to Canadian culture and wanted to create something resonant for them. As well, 2 designers on the team were alumni and they were very keen to design something that they could feel proud of as designers as well as alumni.

**Nowadays, more and more logo projects are not restricted within one logo. Instead, series of logos are designed for a project. What do you think of this trend of logo design?**

It will be interesting to see if this is a trend or if it is simply the way we now design for this digital world. The platforms for design work, identities included, are no longer primarily print applications. We now design for applications that are often fluid, in motion, unfixed. We have a sense of brands as living things – they change just as we do – and reflecting that in identity design work seems to make sense.

:Diversity

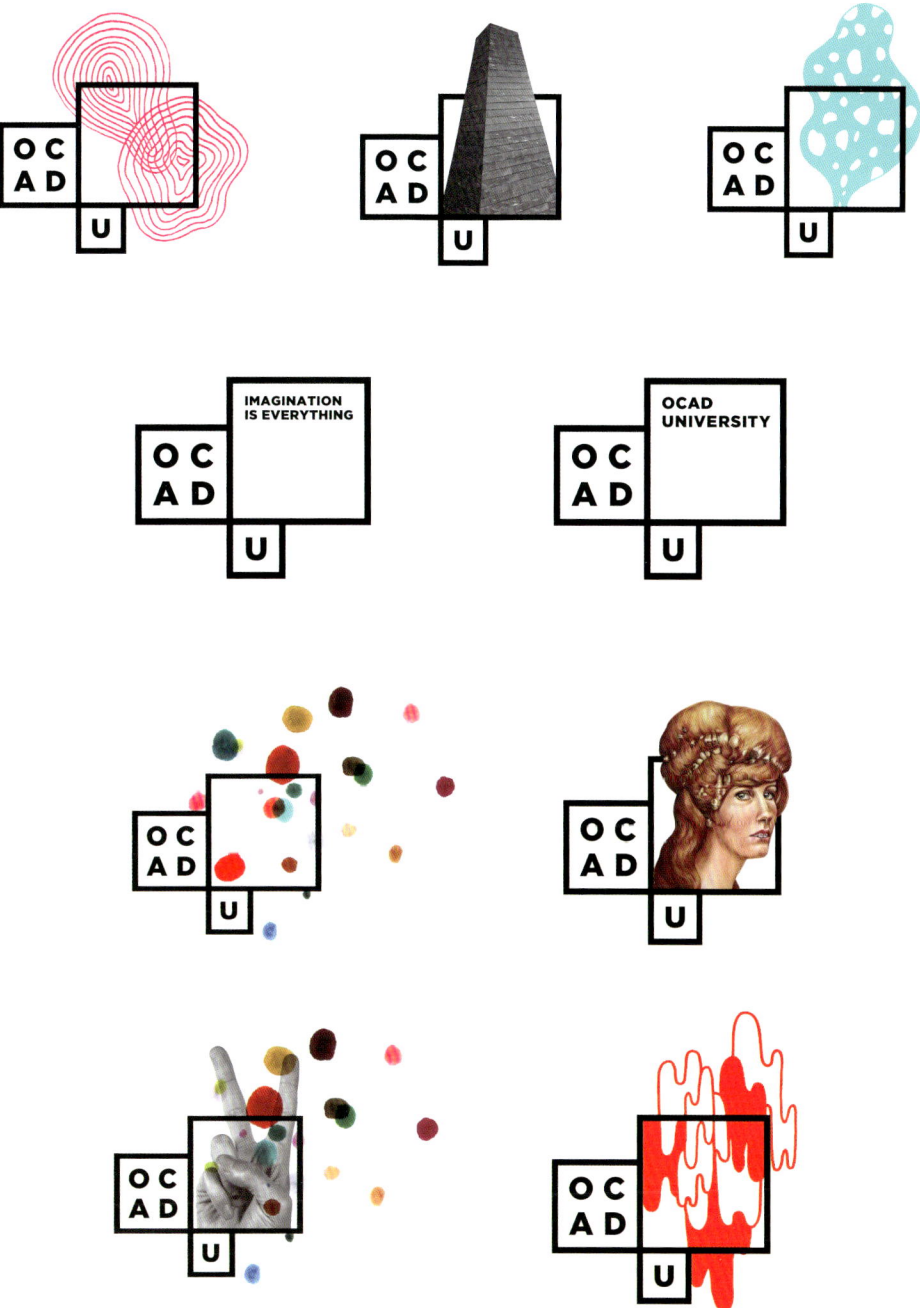

:Diversity

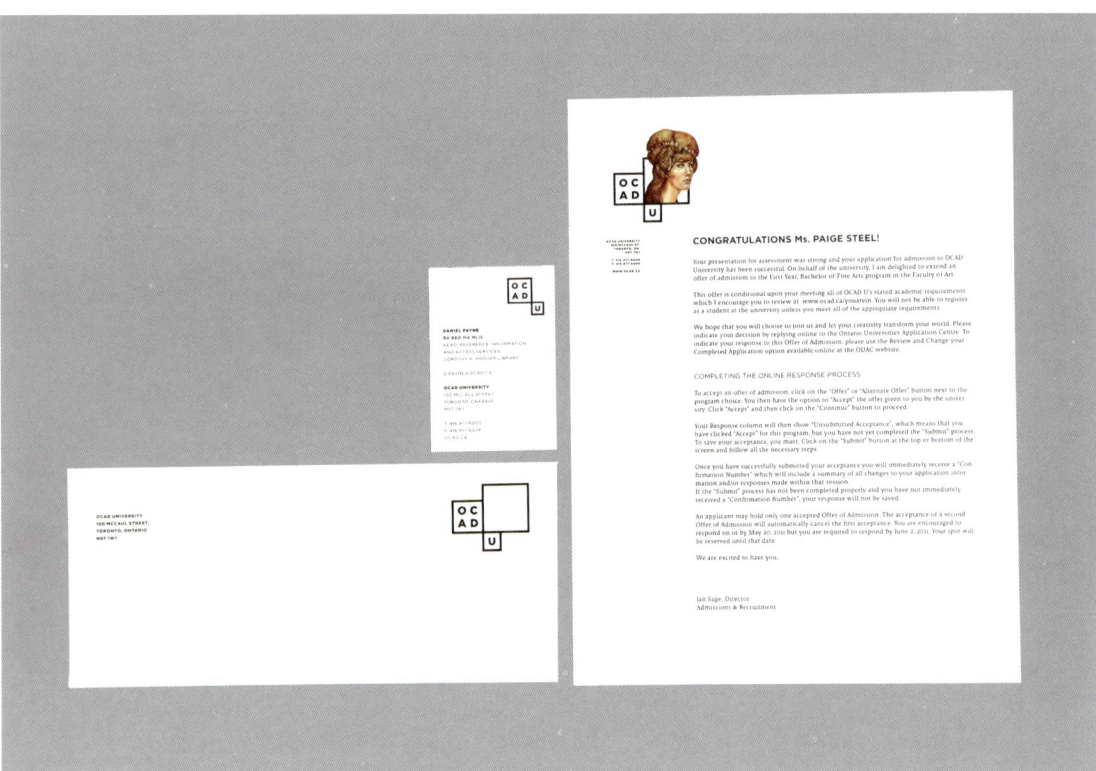

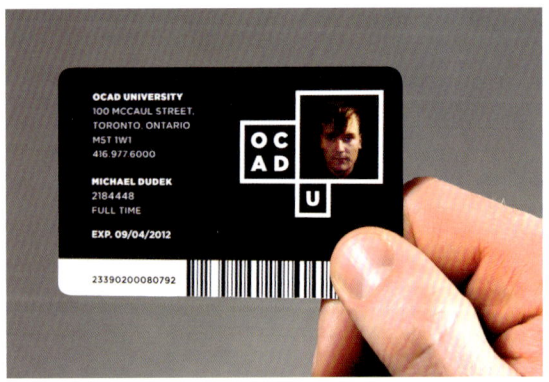

:Diversity

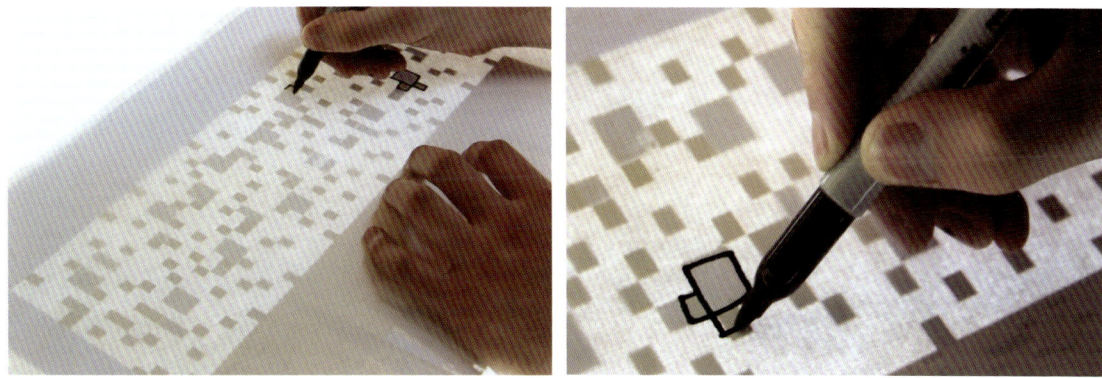

:Diversity

04 GXY Search

# GXYsearch

04

Truly Deeply has recently been working with Australia's leading specialist Gen Y recruitment brand. Truly Deeply provided GXY Search absolute clarity around their market proposition and layers of brand definition to allow them to align and focus their brand and business activities. As it often does, this new-found clarity of the brand led to a brief to update the GXY brand identity.

From sport to fashion, lifestyle to advertising, GXY's clients all boast "excitement jobs" – the type of jobs many Gen Yers dream about. One of the defining attributes of Gen Y is they see themselves as distinct individuals who belong to a range of overlapping tribes. GXY genuinely has a right to lead those tribes as it is authentically Gen Y itself, from the way it thinks to how it behaves and where it parties, GXY is Gen Y through and through. The brand identity was a reflection of their own status within the Gen Y tribes they belong to. The brand identity concept was developed through Truly Deeply's creative brand design process. The brand identity developed was applied to business stationery, interior design and website.

:Diversity

05 5 Sentits                                06 328 Stories

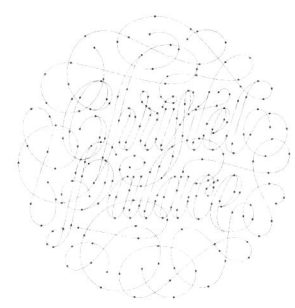

05
:Client's Brief
5 Sentits is a store and café which dedicated to the latest Scandinavian design.

:Design Philosophy
In the name 5 Sentits, there are two parts, one is quantity/number and the other one is value/message. The first one is the most interesting, because it promotes and heads the name, and allows growing the corporate message. 5 was put to serve the message and to make to grow the possibilities and / or needs of communication of the new resultant brand. A symbol was made based on the concept of communication and constant innovation in the same emblem. The aim is to identify the brand with facility.

06
:Client's Brief
328 Stories wanted to develop a new identity which shows the variety of people and skills within their company.

:Design Philosophy
328 Stories works together with all kinds of storytellers: film directors, graphic designers, photographers, bloggers. Part of a Bigger Plan developed an ever-changing identity in which each logo is a story in itself aiming for 328 logos a year. That's 328 Stories waiting to be made.

:Diversity

07 Berrys of Holborn

08 Moreton Bay & Islands

Berrys of Holborn Ltd

07
:Client's Brief
Berrys of Holborn are a well established firm providing maintenance and repairs to office equipment. They contacted Superfried to help them refresh their dated look.

:Design Philosophy
Although well established, Superfried felt the first issue was the company name since new potential customers will be oblivious to the nature of their business. To address this issue Superfried developed a logo that demonstrates the actual product they repair in fine working order.

08
:Client's Brief
The aim was to create one unified visual and verbal identity for the Queensland's Moreton Bay & Islands region.

:Design Philosophy
Referencing the popular "cluster" of beautiful, unspoiled islands (and subtly housing the "more than" symbol) the logo mark is used not only as an identifier, but also is abstracted to form the basis of the "more to..."verbal identity.

:Diversity

09 Ookla

09
:Client's Brief
Ookla is the global leader in broadband speed testing and web-based network diagnostic applications. The company is growing strongly and in need of the new branding to reflect the direction of the brand.

:Design Philosophy
"Ookla" is already a fun name to start with, TNOP immediately thought that the simple custom type design with a twist should reflect the energy and the business nature of the company very well. So the "Racing Stripes" concept was chosen to represent the company in a more fun and dynamic way.

:Diversity

10 IVA

10
:Client's Brief
The perception of the school and the work of its graduates had not kept pace with the times. Especially in Denmark, the institution was seen as old fashioned. The reality was that the school operated in a complex and rapidly-developing field that was being transformed by technology and new demands for information. A new identity was needed to clarify its work and clearly position itself while differentiating from educational competitors.

:Design Philosophy
A new visual identity was introduced in 2010 that captured the new brand positioning and name change. The brandmark was based on the Fibonacci sequence which is employed across the boundaries of art, science and mathematics. It was supported with a flexible visual system that incorporates imagery from the ever-expanding fields of human knowledge.

:Diversity

:Diversity

11 Your Singapore.com

# UNIQUELY
# Singapore
## www.visitsingapore.com

11
:Client's Brief
BBH Asia Pacific launched YourSingapore.com, a groundbreaking new brand campaign for the Singapore Tourism Board (STB). This global campaign evolves STB's previous brand "Uniquely Singapore" into a new phase that puts digital at the heart of its marketing.

:Design Philosophy
The new STB Destination Brand Logo eschews conventional wisdom of what a logo should be or how it should behave; it is a logo that never looks the same way twice, ever-evolving and dynamic – just like Singapore. These logos represent the many facets of Singapore visitors have come to know and love. Each facet, seen on its own, is called a Thematic Logo. In cases where it's theme-neutral, BBH use the Master Logo.

The "Master Logo" is the one with pink, red, purple and blue overlapping cubes aiming at suggesting multiplicity and a concentration of offerings. The rest of the logos are the Thematic Logos.

:Diversity

:Diversity

## [12] Custom Color Corp

**What does your client want to achieve through redesigning the logo?**

Custom Color Corp was looking for a fresh new logo that reflected their hardworking and fun personality. They wanted something that communicated what they did and differentiated them from their competitors.

**Compared to the old logo, the new one seems to be much more lovely and approachable, why did you redesign it this way?**

We wanted to create a logo that was friendly, modern and timeless. The "C" drop and the ink-head characters allowed our client to have both a corporate side and a more consumer friendly presence.

**How did you come up with the idea of employing CMYK as the concept and theme color of the entire identity?**

We were inspired by the printing process itself which uses 4 ink colors: Cyan, Magenta, Yellow and Black. Limiting ourselves to this color palette allowed us to be as creative as possible with the application while still conveying the nature of our clients service.

**Being simple and concise is one of the trend of logo design nowadays. The new logo seems to be of this kind. Is designing simple and concise logo your design philosophy all along?**

A company's logo should communicate the essence of the company at a glance. In this case, the ink droplet and the letter C was the perfect combination.

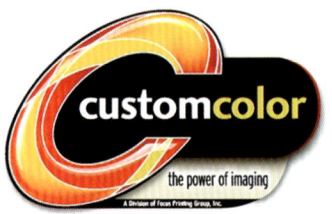

:Diversity

:Diversity

### [13] Belmacz

Belmacz is a London based jewelry company who will open its first shop and gallery in London Mayfair soon. For this reason Mind Design re-designed the original identity and worked in collaboration with Jump Studios on the interior.

The new identity takes the original logo (which has been in use for about 8 years) but adds a variety of thicker, "raw" letter shapes. Those shapes relate to the process in which raw minerals and diamonds are more and more refined until they become a piece of jewelry. The visual references start with the mines, go to the raw materials, the raw letter shapes and in the end to the refined letter shapes of the original logo.

Mining is a brutal intervention with the environment where often massive holes are "cut out" of the earth. The conditions under which people work in mines for example in Africa or Siberia are hard and their life could not be more different from that of the rich clientele shopping in Mayfair.

On their journey from the mine to the jewelry shop in mayfair the materials go through many hands and constantly change location. Not only the raw materials travel also the final pieces of jewelry are often passed on from one generation to the next, given away as presents, get stolen or auctioned. It was important to visualise this idea of dislocation and constant travel. The new Belmacz identity is a complex system of connections and works across many different items and media. Every shape that has been cut out on one item of communication re-appears on another. For example a shape missing on a business card can re-appear on a carrier bag.

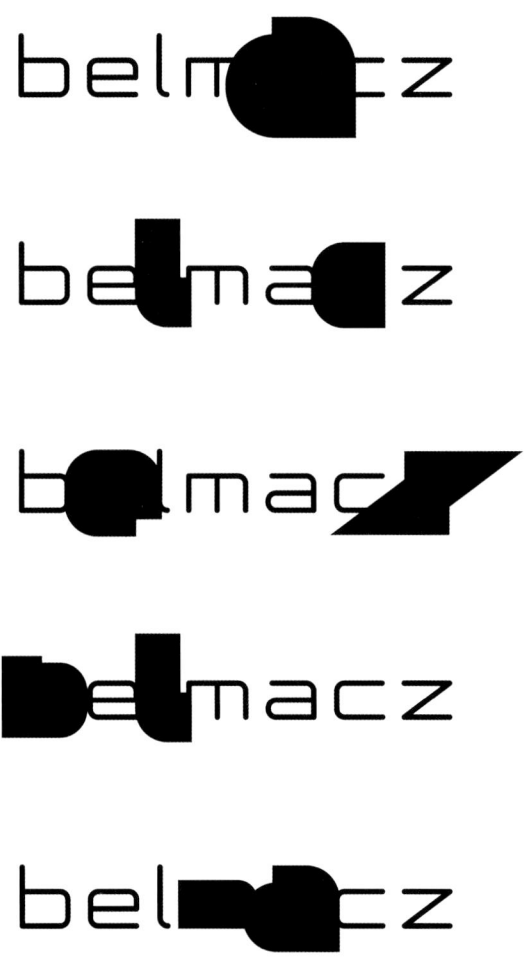

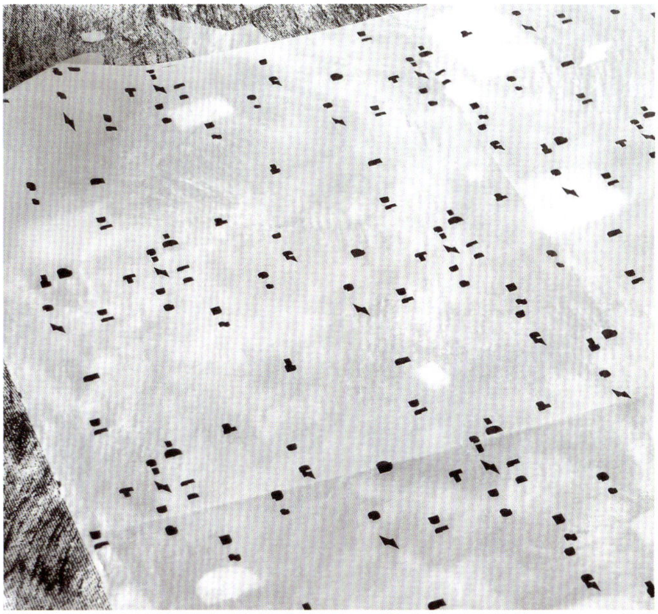

:Diversity

:Diversity

## The Hungarian University of Fine Arts

**What is your client's requirement on the redesign?**
In late spring, 2011, the Hungarian University of Fine Arts decided to renew its identity. They didn't want to abandon the old mark's philosophy which comes from the form. The shields are the symbol of the guardian saint of art. When it all started, the university was an academy and had only three departments. So this is why the three shields. The school has used this mark from the very beginning so in the brief it was a must to somehow keep the old logo to provide continuity. 125 years later the university now has seven departments. The brief said to come up with a solution to differentiate these. To sum up, create a new mark from the old that is suitable to represent all the departments.

**The shapes of the logo are varied. What's the concept of developing a series of different logos? What do the different shapes represent?**
I've redrawn the shapes of the shields and pushed them together to create interesting forms. These forms reminds people of the drawing studies of cubic shapes and distinct three dimensional objects, which refers to the importance of drawing studies at the university. The three shields could be combined in different ways, so we have several different marks. Every department has it's own combination. These forms are identical to each other but also different. By using all the marks is a great way to differentiate the seven departments while maintaining coherence.

**Why did you use black and yellow as the theme color of the new logo?**
Black is the color of pencils, pens and inks. This is the color with which bold, strong marks could have been drawn. Black is also serious which comes handy for a prestigious university. And black which every color could be paired with. Yellow came from the interior. Very beautiful patterns decorate the main building. All the way down gilded frescos, brownish and yellowish murals. So yellow was an obvious choice.

**From your professional point of view, are there any durable logos? Or do the logos need to meet with time changes?**
I think there are a lot of timeless marks out there. If a logo is really well designed than in the first instance it is deliberate. Those logos that I think are durable, and the ones that have a good idea and use a very straight-forward simple graphical language to communicate that idea. These will meet with time changes because they are free of any trends and styles.

**What do you and your client think of the end result?**
I think the solution is fresh and pointing to a new direction but also carrying the roots. By creating a dynamic mark it will serve well when – for example – a new department would be set up. This is a flexible system that could be used across a wide range of media.

:Diversity

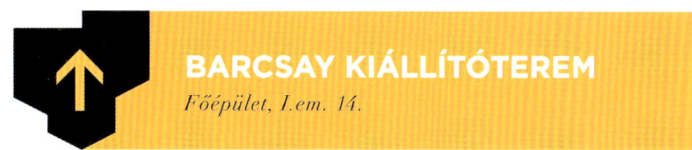

:Diversity

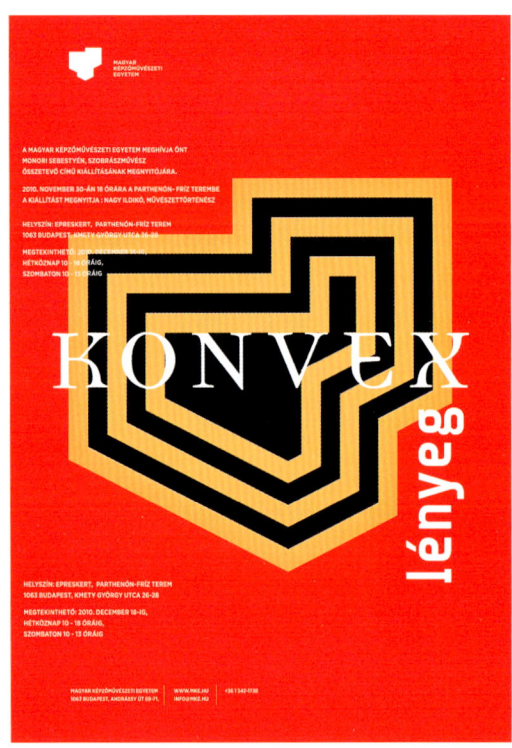

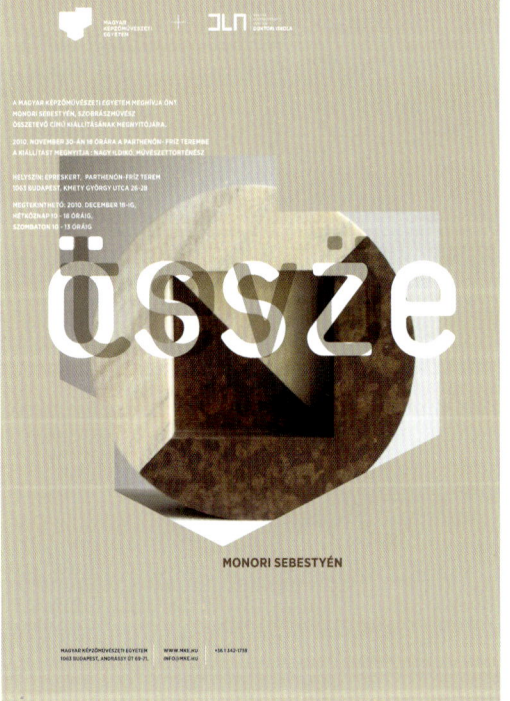

:Diversity

15 GloryHoleMusic

15
:Client's Brief
Superfried were asked by their friends at GloryHoleMusic to rebrand and refresh the marketing material for their club night GloryHole. This was a challenging brief since the style of music played can vary greatly in a single event.

:Design Philosophy
As a consequence Superfried needed to create a template structure that was rigid and distinct to maintain brand strength / awareness whilst ensuring versatility to adapt to any genre of music or venue. The answer, as so often the case in design, was simplicity. The name itself suggested a circle so that is what Superfried used as a focal point. The circle was simple, but offered infinite possibilities. This property then led to the development of the "infinity" connecting device and "wings" within the logo. Lastly symmetry was utlised to reinforce distinction.

:Diversity

:Diversity

:Diversity

## [16] VPRO

**What does the client hope to achieve through redesigning the logo?**

The VPRO is one of 17 broadcasting companies that fill the three public TV channels in The Netherlands. They are the most intellectual and free-minded of the 17. With the new identity the VPRO tries to show in a clearer way which programmes are theirs.

**What inspired you to create this logo? And what did you consider the most when redesigning the logo?**

We kept what was good about the 30-year-old logo, to achieve a sense of continuity, but we opened the logo up in more than one way. We saw the typographic image of v-p-r-o not as an end form, but as a beginning, the beginning of a typeface and the beginning of a play in variation. We have more than a billion variations now to use on several media and subjects.

**You have developed a series of variations of the logo. And color is the main factor of the variations. Could you explain the color scheme of this project?**

Because of the amount of different faces the VPRO has, we wanted the logo to be as flexible as possible.

Therefore a lot of color combinations are available, as long as it is bright and vivid.

**Geometric figure seems to be another main factor of the logo. Do you frequently apply geometric figures in your design? And why?**

Geometric figures are abstract but are open to a lot of meanings. They can become icons if used in the right way.

Their simplicity makes it interesting to play with and it can form an multiple identity in the end.

**Nowadays, more and more logo projects are not restricted within one logo. Instead, series of logos are designed for a project. What do you think of this trend of logo design?**

For the VPRO it works really well, because a lot of people work with this company, and even more people know the TV-broadcaster a long time.

From that point of view the VPRO is almost a person, and with the logo system it shows its different character traits.

We don't focus on trends, a good design is based on content.

:Diversity

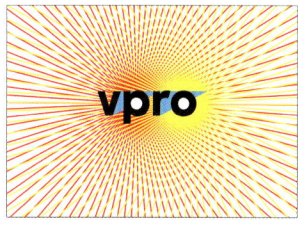

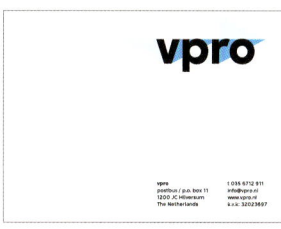

255

:Diversity

## [17] Fish Don't Dance

Superfried were asked by their friends at international club night "Fish Don't Dance", to develop the brand and a new marketing scheme. Working with the existing logo, Superfried decided that the "fish" should be the star of the show. For each new event the fish would feature centre stage on the flyers and posters in a new guise. This provided Superfried with great creative freedom using mediums such as lego, ketchup, illustration, spray paint, photography and toast! Logos and typography were kept to a minimum to reduce intrusion on the artwork. To facilitate this, distinct container devices were developed for the FDD and venue logos. With the rebrand in place Superfried carried this styling through the development of their website.

:Diversity

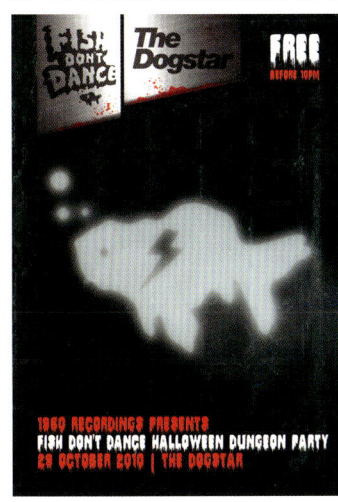

:Diversity

18 Heesterveld

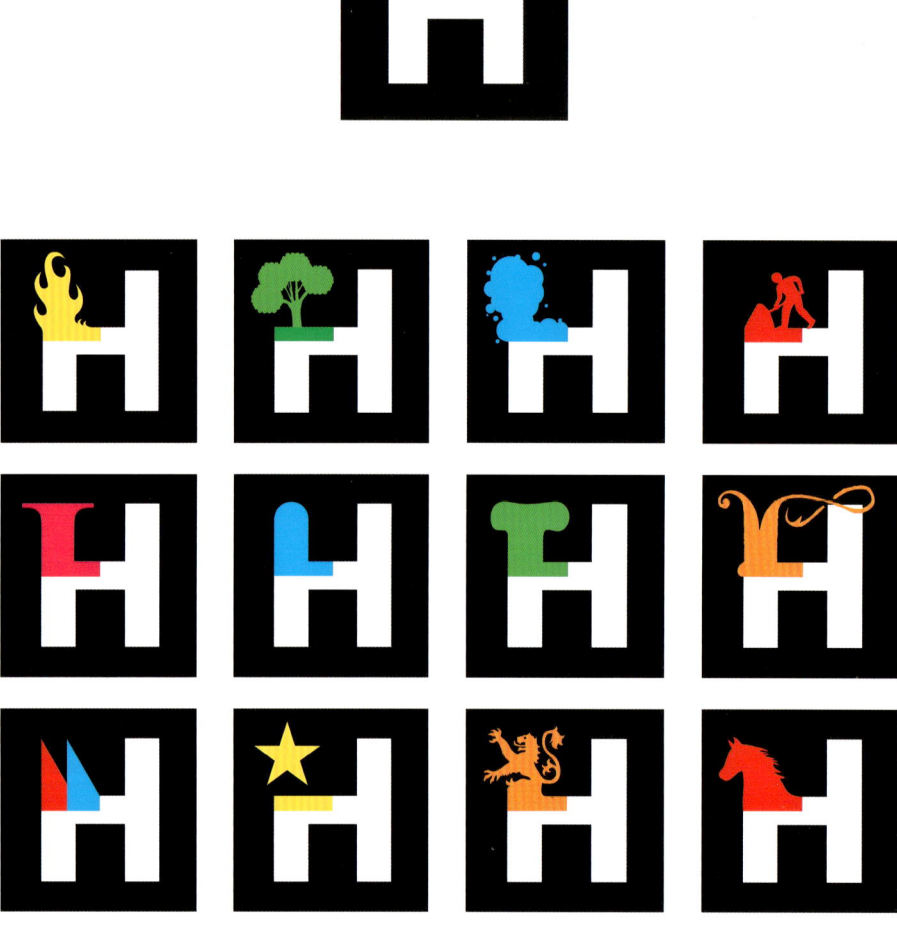

18
:Client's Brief
Heestrveld wanted to have an identity which can show the diversity of the project, the usage of the building estate.

:Design Philosophy
The first "quarter" of the existing logo is used to show diversity of the usage of the building estate.

:Diversity

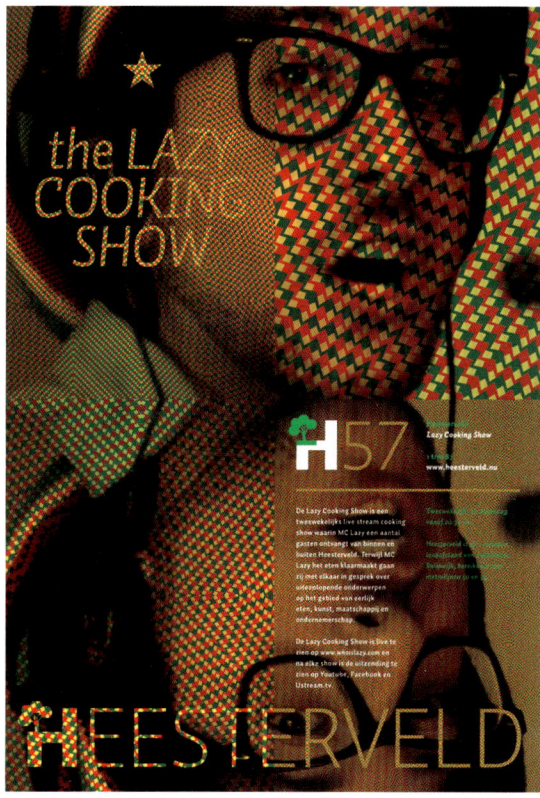

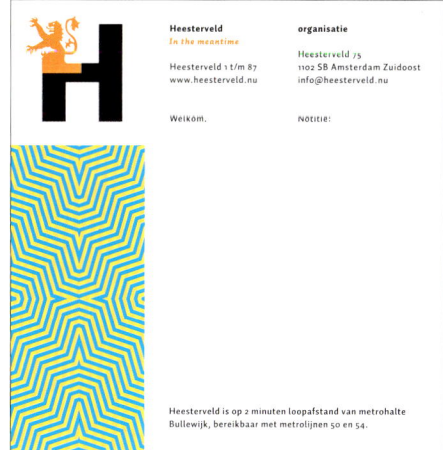

:Diversity

19 Nike 5

**19**
**:Client's Brief**
Nike 5 logo was as a base but needed to be made more African and more communicating the event by transforming it. It needed to be visually concentrated in the middle.

**:Design Philosophy**
The big 5 of African safari (the animals) is used to illuminate the existing logo. A more visual striking version was created to use in the campaign.

20 The Tracks

# THE**TRACKS**

20
:Client's Brief
The Tracks is a blog focused on music, bands, DJs, musicians, concerts, festivals, record labels and any other music-related stuff. Elegant and progressive logo was needed at the same time.

:Design Philosophy
The name was shortened from "The Tracks" to the progressive "Tracks". The branding potential was enhanced with a remarkable logo design that reminded of musical notes.

# :DESIGNER INDEX

Singapore
&Larry
034-035, 144-146
andlarry.com

Denmark
1508
198
1508.dk

## A

Singapore
Adventure
208:126
adventureadvertising.com

USA
Alex Lin
124
alexlin.org

Germany
Andre Weier
259
nalindesign.com

Andy Baron
148
andy-baron.com

USA
Anti/Anti
138
antiantinyc.com

## B

Spain
BAG
237:05
bagdisseny.com

France
BAYADERES
109:135, 152:36
bayaderes.fr

BBH Asia Pacific
242-243
bbh.co.uk

Sweden
Become
083:99
become.se

Switzerland
Blackswan
036, 037:20, 077
black-s.ch

Switzerland
blue-infinity
165:61
b-i.com

Italy
Blumagenta
209:129, 222:153
blumagenta.com

Poland
BNA
057:57, 156:43, 176:77
bna.pl

Sweden
Bo Lundberg
073
bolundberg.com

Romania
Brandient
060:65, 098-99, 140:22, 153, 156:44
brandient.com

Canada
Bruce Mau Design
232-233
brucemaudesign.com

Malta
Bulldog
196-197
virtualbulldog.com

UK
Bunch
037:19, 190
bunchdesign.com

The Netherlands
Buro Reng
120-121, 122-123, 177, 215:141
buroreng.nl

Singapore
BÜRO UFHO
071:82
ufho.com

## C

USA
C&G Partners
176:76, 078, 186:95, 219:146, 222:151, 224:157
cgpartnersllc.com

USA
CA Square
203
ca-square.com

The Netherlands
Calango
038:21, 050:48, 157:45, 202:119, 211:133
calango.nl

Portugal
Carlos Ribeiro
139:20
sevenfiles.com

Australia
Canvas Group
026, 066:69, 083:98, 088, 147
canvasgroup.com.au

Switzerland
Caselli Associates
126:03, 159:50,51, 166
caselli.ch

USA
Chermayeff & Geismar
066:71, 090:109, 127, 160:53, 200:115, 201:116
cgstudionyc.com

Greece
Chris Trivizas
167:64
christrivizas.gr

The Netherlands
CLEVER°FRANKE
065
cleverfranke.com

Japan
Commune
141-143
commune-inc.jp

UK
Company
058:59, 060:64, 192:106
company-london.com

Ireland
Creative Inc.
070:79, 097:123, 201:118
creativeinc.ie

## D

Spain
David Torrents
059:61
torrents.info

Italy
Demetrio Mancini
079:95
demetriomancini.it

USA
Design Ranch
072:84, 106, 151:31, 214, 244-245
design-ranch.com

Norway
Designers Journey
170:70, 212, 213:137
designersjourney.com

Spain
di-da komunikakzioa
037:18, 072:83, 085
di-da.com

Sweden
Dolhem Design
089:107, 092:116
dolhemdesign.se

The Netherlands
DTM_INC
139:21, 158:49, 169:69, 179:82
behance.net/dtm_inc

USA
Duffy & Partners
033:15, 076:88, 107:130, 126:02, 139:19, 151:32, 208:127
duffy.com

Duval Guillaume Corporate
038:23, 047:43, 161:57
duvalguillaume.com

## E

Denmark
Ekaterina Tiouleikina
061, 068
itchyorange.com

The Netherlands
El Miro
040:28
elmiro.nl

Scotland
El Studio
024:02, 071:81
el-studio.co.uk

USA
Entermotion Design Studio
161:56
entermotion.com

USA
Erik Kiesewetter
110:138, 135:16, 215:140
erikbelowsealevel.com

USA
Established
027:08, 102-105
establishednyc.com

Switzerland
Esther Rieser
114-115
estr.ch

New Zealand
Everything Design
039:24, 211:135
everythingdesign.co.nz

# F

German
F1RSTDESIGN
202:121
f1rstdesign.com

UK
Figtree
154:04
figtreenetwork.com

Germany
Floor5
033:14
floor5.de

The Netherlands
Floor Wesseling
130, 179:83, 183:89, 090, 222:152, 258-259, 260
floorwesseling.nl

Brazil
Friedrich Santana Lamego
180:85, 184:91, 092
elesefe.com

# G

USA
Garrett Patz
110:137
cogniform.com

Gaston Yagmourian
148, 158:48
Yagmourian.com/gaston

Norway
Grandpeople
174-175
grandpeople.org

Switzerland
GVA Studio
047:44, 058:60, 067:72
gvastudio.com

# H

China
HALLUCINATE
110:136
hallucinate.com.cn

Norway
Haltenbanken
038:22, 125:153, 151:33
haltenbanken.com

Denmark
Henrik Gytz
184:93
gytz.com

Mexico
HULA + HULA
056:53, 179:81, 180:84
hulahula.com.mx

USA
Hyperakt
093:118
hyperakt.com

# I

Romania
Inpublic
069:77
inpublic.ro

Interbrand
091:112, 101, 150, 168, 192:104, 238:08
interbrand.com

Switzerland
Inventaire
041:31, 208:128
inventaire.ch

# J

USA
Jeff Fisher LogoMotives
089:108
jfisherlogomotives.com

Italy
jekyll & hyde
211:134
jeh.it

The Netherlands
John Beckers
054-055
john-beckers.nl

Australia
Just Creative Design
050:49
justcreativedesign.com

# K

Greece
Kanella Arapoglou
157:46, 161:55
kanella.com

Ken Frederick
148
Cargocollective.com/kenfrederick

Ukraine
Konovalov.XCLV
091:113, 194-195
xclv.com

# L

Landor
128-129, 228-231
landor.com

Spain
Lavernia & Cienfuegos Design
069:75
lavernia-cienfuegos.com

Lippincott
091:114, 093:119, 152:35, 224:156
lippincott.com

Canada
Liquid Agency
154:39, 155, 181, 224:158
liquidagency.com

# M

Denmark
Make®
024:04, 074-75, 209:130, 240-241
make.dk

UK
Mammal
090:111, 188
mammaldesign.com

Mexico
MANIFIESTO FUTURA
033:13, 044:37, 134:12
manifiestofutura.com

UK
Mark Lawson Bell Studio
136-137
marklawsonbell.co.uk

Argentina
másSustancia
047:42, 170:72
massustancia.com

USA
Matthew Manos
202:120
mattmanos.com

Mexico
Memoma
086-087
memoma.tv

MetaDesign
040:27, 160:54
metadesign.com

Australia
Minale Tattersfield
059:62
minale.com.au

UK
Mind Design
246-247
minddesign.co.uk

Venezuela
Modo
048, 049
modovisual.com

Spain
Morillas
024:03, 027:07, 043:35, 044:39, 084:101, 102, 092:117, 140:24, 165:62
morillas.com

Australia
Moving Brands
133, 160
movingbrands.com

France
Murmure
025, 080-081, 134:13, 167:65
murmure.me

# N

Argentina
Negro™
056:54, 096, 169:68, 187:98,99
negronouveau.com

Norway
Neue Design Studio
028-029
neue.no

Sweden
Nicklas Hultman
213:138
nicklas-h.se

Argentina
NNSS
100, 172-173, 210:132, 223:155
nnss.com.ar

Poland
Noeeko
191, 204
noeeko.com

# O

Belgium
OBLIQUE
113, 141
oblq.be

Switzerland
onlab
162-163
onlab.ch

USA
OVO
089:106
brandsbyovo.com

# P

Croatia
Parabureau
225
parabureau.com

The Netherlands
Part of a Bigger Plan
237:06
part of a bigger plan.com

UK
Proekt Communication Agency
108
proekt.co.uk

Thailand
Prompt Design
058:58
prompt-design.com

UK
Proud Creative
067:73, 070:80, 156:42
proudcreative.com

UK
Purpose
079:93, 084:100, 134:14, 164, 199:112
purpose.co.uk

# R

Australia
R-Co
060:63, 132:08,09,10, 216-217
r-co.com.au

Italy
R&MAG
069: 76, 070:78
remag.it

Belgium
Raf Vancampenhoudt
039:25,26
rafvancampenhoudt.be

Italy
RAINERI DESIGN
076:89,90, 097:122, 154:38
raineridesign.com

Norway
Renata Barros
118-119
renatabarros.net

China
Resonance
220, 221:148,149,150
resonance.cn

USA
RoAndCo
107:132, 169:67
roanneadams.com

Spain
Rocío Martinavarro
131
rociomartinavarro.es

# S

Saffron Consultants
183:88
saffron-consultants.com

USA
Sagmeister Inc.
022-023, 085
sagmeister.com

Slovenia
Saša Stucin
079:94, 112, 117:146
sasa.stucin@gmail.com

USA
Siegel+Gale
218:143, 219:145
siegelgale.com

UK
SomeOne
111, 170:71, 182
someoneinlondon.com

Canada
Sorachief Design Ltd.
117:145
sorachief.com

Australia
Studio Brave
158:47
studiobrave.com.au

Czech
Stas Sipovich
192:105, 199:111
sipovich.com

Hungary
Studio Borzak
248-250
martonborzak.com

UK
Studio Hansa
178
studiohansa.com

UK
Studio Fla
027:09
studiofla.com

UK
Studio Output
109:134, 126:01, 186:96, 187:99
studio-output.com

UK
superfried design
042, 052-053, 078, 189, 193, 238:07, 251-253, 256-257
superfried.com

# T

The Brand Union
092:115, 165:60
thebrandunion.com

USA
The Original Champions of Design
062-064
originalchampionsofdesign.com

Switzerland
Thomas Hirter
041:30, 043:34,36, 066:70, 200:113
thomashirter.ch

The Netherlands
Thonik
254-255
thonikbyyou.com

Denmark
Tim Bjørn
218:144
timbjorn.com

TNOP™ DESIGN
117:147, 171, 239
tnop.com

USA
TomTor Studio
094-095, 125:152, 205, 206-207
tomtor.com

Australia
Truly Deeply
030-031, 107:131, 149, 236
trulydeeply.com.au

UK
Turner Duckworth
040:29, 041:32, 057:56, 090:110, 135:15, 140:23, 152:34, 201:117
turnerduckworth.com

## U

Spain
Unlimited Creative Group
097:124
unlimitedcreativegroup.com

## V

UK
venturethree
032, 045, 046, 226-227
venturethree.com

France
Vivien Le Jeune Durhin
050:47
vivienlejeunedurhin.com

## W

Belgium
We Love Moules Frites
113:142, 116
welovemoulesfrites.com

Wolff Olins
200:114
wolffolins.com

## X

Spain
Xose Teiga Studio
082
xoseteiga.com

## Y

UK
Yolo Ltd.
185
yolo.info

## Z

Slovenia
Zek Crew
051
zek.si

# :WORK INDEX

a. Agency
cd. Creative Director
ad. Art Director
d. Designer
p. Photographer
t. Typography
i. Illustrator
c. Copywriter
pp. Print Production

**189:1980 Recordings**
a. superfried design

**237.06:328 stories**
a. Rens Wegerif

**214:360 Architecture**
a. Design Ranch

**237.05:5 Sentits**
a. BAG

**128:9/11 Memorial Museum**
a. Landor

## A

**198:Aarhus University**
a. 1508
d. Tore Rosbo, Clea Simonsen

**165:60:Airtel**
a. The Brand Union

**022-023:AÏSHTI**
a. Sagmeister Inc.
ad. Stefan Sagmeister
d. Jessica Walsh, Joe Shouldice, Jong Woo Si
p. Bela Borsodi, Henry Hargreaves
i. Jonathan Puckey, Jessica Walsh
pp. Jonathan Puckey, Jessica Walsh, Michael Freimuth

**085:AÏZONE**
a. Sagmeister Inc.
ad. Stefan Sagmeister
d. Jessica Walsh, Joe Shouldice, Jong Woo Si
p. Bela Borsodi, Henry Hargreaves
i. Jonathan Puckey, Jessica Walsh
pp. Jonathan Puckey, Jessica Walsh, Michael Freimuth

**068:Alg Börje**
a. Ekaterina Tiouleikina

**219.146:Alhurra**
a. C&G Partners

**192.106:Almo**
a. Company

**171:Alongkorn**
a. TNOP™ DESIGN

**90.110:Amazon.com**
a. Turner Duckworth
cd. David Turner, Bruce Duckworth
ad. Sarah Moffat
d. Britt Hull, Tanawat Pisanuwongse, Kearney McDonnell

**202.119:Amsterdam Student Festival**
a. Calango

**037.18:Anboto**
a. di-da komunikakzioa

**113.141:Anthony-And**
a. OBLIQUE

**183.88:Apollo**
a. Saffron Consultants
cd. Mike Abbink
d. Mike Abbink, Josh Distler, Jodie Gatlin

**140.23:Applegate**
a. Turner Duckworth
cd. David Turner, Bruce Duckworth
ad. Sarah Moffat
d. Britt Hull, Tanawat Pisanuwongse, Kearney McDonnell

**159.50:Arema**
a. Caselli Associates

**079.94:Armada**
a. Saša Stucin

**066.71:Armani Exchange**
a. Chermayeff & Geismar

**091.113:Artcapital**
a. Konovalov.XCLV

**025:ArtComArt**
a. Murmure

**058.58:Asian Clay Shooting Federation**
a. Prompt Design

**152.36:Aster**
a. BAYADERES
cd. Annabelle Brietzke, Charlotte Vallee

**154.39:Aviat**
a. Liquid Agency
cd. Boyd Tveit

**192.104:Award**
a. Interbrand

## B

**165.62:Barcelona Tribuna**
a. Morillas

**206-207:Basement Media**
a. TomTor Studio

**136-137:BB's**
a. Mark Lawson Bell

**184.92:Beat-Army.org**
a. Friedrich Santana Lamego

**246-247:Belmacz**
a. Mind Design

**200.113:Bern**
d. Thomas Hirter

**238.07:Berrys of Holborn**
a. superfried design

**177:Biblionet ID**
a. Buro Reng

**211.134:Bike Ribbon**
a. jekyll & hyde

**051:BIKOFE**
a. Zek Crew

**211.133:Binc**
a. Calango

**069.77:Biostase**
a. Inpublic
ad. Andrei Botez

**167.65:Bistrot Gourmand**
a. Murmure

**130:Blood in Blood out**
a. Floor Wesseling

**048:Black Magic Sound**
a. Modo

**102-105:Blow**
a. Established

**024.02:BMJ Architects**
a. El Studio

**114-115:Bolsopaseo**
a. El Studio

**056.54:Bombo**
a. Negro™

**049:Boogie Nights**
a. Modo

**1.112:bpost**
a. Interbrand
cd. Andy Payne, Markus Blankenburg, Thierry Bigard
d. Jean-Jaques Charrais, Claire-Jean Engelmann

**176.77:Brainville**
a. BNA

**154.38:Bresciani**
a. RAINERI DESIGN

**079.95:Brosway**
d. Demetrio Mancini, Nando Landi

**151.33:BTO**
a. Haltenbanken

## C

**038.21:Calango**
a. Calango
d. Jeroen Krielaars (Calango), Sandra Gutkin (Sandragutkin)

**196-197:Calleja**
a. Bulldog
d. Ren Spiteri

**170.70:Canvas Group**
a. Canvas Group

**033.14:Caras Gourmet**
a. Floor5

**155:CareerBliss**
a. Liquid Agency
cd. Boyd Tveit

**194-195:CDMA**
a. Konovalov.XCLV

**096:Cehba**
a. Negro™

**070.78:Centro Laser**
a. R&MAG

**200.115:Chase Manhattan Bank**
a. Chermayeff & Geismar

**110.136:Cheung Ning**
a. HALLUCINAT

**141-143:Chicken Pecker**
a. Commune
ad. Ryo Ueda
d. Ryo Ueda, Minami Mabuchi, Natsumi Oguma, Daisuke Takada, Yuji Terada, Kazuki Murata
p. Takuto Kosukegawa
c. Kosuke Ikehata
pp. Takaaki Tsukada

**228-231:City of Melbourne**
a. Landor
cd. Jason Little
ad. Jason Little
d. Jefton Sungkar, Jason Little, Sam Pemberton, Ivana Martinovic, Malin Holmstrom
p. Joao Peres, Chenying Hao
c. Kosuke Ikehata

**059.62:City of Randwick**
a. Minale Tattersfield

**070.80:Clear Channel International**
a. Proud Creative

**135.15:Coca-Cola Freestyle**
a. Turner Duckworth
cd. David Turner, Bruce Duckworth
ad. Sarah Moffat
d. Rebecca Williams

**134.13:Comédie De Reims**
a. Murmure

**127:Conservation International**
a. Chermayeff & Geismar

**218.143:CooperVision**
a. Siegel+Gale

**069.76:Corso 9**
a. R&MAG

**187.99:Club 18-30**
a. Studio Output

**199.112:CPA**
a. Purpose

**135.16:Creative Alliance of New Orleans**
d. Erik Kiesewetter

**092.117:Crèdit Andorrà**
a. Morillas

208.126:Creative Memories
a. Adventure
cd. Karen Thompson (Creative Memories)
ad. Corinne Skoog (Creative Memories), Rick Jensen (Adenvure), Jon Loss (Adventure), Abby Fitch (Adventure)

132.08:Cricket Victoria
a. R-Co

161.56:Crown 3 Realty
a. Entermotion Design Studio

244-245:Custom Color Corp
a. Design Ranch

## D

215.141:Dag van de Architectuur Groningen
a. Buro Reng

073:Dahl Agenturer
a. Bo Lundberg

176.76:Darien Library
a. C&G Partners

039.24:Dasko
a. Everything Design

169.69:DD Design
a. DTM_INC

091.114:Delta
a. Lippincott
cd. Connie Birdsall
d. Adam Stringer, Kevin Hammond, Michael Milligan, Fabian Diaz

218.144:DermaMed Solutions
d. Tim Bjørn

072.84:Design Ranch
a. Design Ranch

204:Design Wars
a. Noeeko

116:Dethier Architectures
a. We Love Moules Frites

180.85:DID Records
d. Friedrich Santana Lamego

076.90:Distillerie Franciacorta
a. RAINERI DESIGN

193:DJ Dan McKie
a. superfried design

042:DJ Will Clarke
a. Superfried Design

041.32:Dolby
a. Turner Duckworth
cd. David Turner, Bruce Duckworth
ad. Shawn Rosenberger
d. Emily Charette, Shawn Rosenberger

098-099:Domo
a. Brandient
d. Cristian 'Kit' Paul, Alin Tamasan, Eugen Erhan

158.49:DTM_INC
a. DTM_INC

179.82:Dubbellistig
a. DTM_INC

097.123:Dublin City Council
a. Creative Inc.

## E

084.100:EFFP
a. Purpose

097.124:Egalsa
a. Unlimited Creative Group

057.87:Empik
a. BNA

072.83:EMUN
a. di-da komunikakzioa

211.135:Endace
a. Everything Design

142.22:Europharm
a. Brandient
d. Bogdan Dumitrache

047.43:Exact
a. Duval Guillaume Corporate
d. Henk Willems

## F

039.25:Fallen
a. Raf Vancampenhoudt

118-119:Fantastic Norway Architects
d. Renata Barros

044.37:Fases
a. MANIFIESTO FUTURA

037.20:Fibrelac
a. Blackswan

132.10:Fire Services
a. R-Co

224.156:First Citizens
a. Lippincott
cd. Connie Birdsall
d. Julia McGreevy, Ippolita Ferrari, Kevin Hammond

066.69:Firstunity
a. Canvas Group

256-257:Fish Don't Dance
a. superfried design

180.84:Fobia
a. Hula + Hula
d. Cha!

208.128:Formul'habitat
a. Inventaire

202.120:Forward Step
cd. Mathew Manos
d. Jessica Lee

088:Fox Johnston
a. Canvas Group

## G

149:Gelati Sky
a. Truly Deeply
cd. David Ansett
ad. David Ansett, Cassandra Gill
d. Cassandra Gill
t. Cassandra Gill
i. Cassandra Gill
Finish Artist: Rachel O'Brien

093.119:Glaad
a. Lippincott
cd. Connie Birdsall
d. Jenifer Lehker, Brendan Murphy, Matt Calkins

060.64:Global Canopy Programme
a. Company

041.31:Globull
a. Inventaire

159.51:Global Encounters
a. Caselli Associates

251-253:GloryHoleMusic
a. superfried design

184.91:Golem
a. Friedrich Santana Lamego

150:Griffin Theatre Company
a. Interbrand

221.149:Guangke Fishery
a. Resonance
d. Dai Fan, Wang Xiaoxue

236:GXY Search
a. Truly Deeply
cd. David Ansett
d. Lachlan McDougall
t. Lachlan McDougall
i. Lachlan McDougall
Finish Artist: Rachel O'Brien

## H

223.155:HakaGroup
a. NNSS
cd. Tomás Fliess
d. Tomás Fliess

199.111:H.A.N.S
d. Stas Sipovich

258-259:Heesterveld
a. Floor Wesseling

213.137:Heimen
a. Designers Journey

056.53:Hello Seahorse
a. Hula + Hula
d. Aldo Lugo

067.72:HEP
a. GVA Studio

076.88:Herradura
a. Duffy & Partners

074-075:Holmegaard
a. Make®
cd. Kristoffer Gudbrand
d. Daniel Flösser, Kristoffer Gudbrand
p. Gunnar Merrild

052-053:HotFridge Records
a. superfried design

154.04:HTC
a. Figtree

065:Hubrecht Institute
a. CLEVER°FRANKE

248-250:Hungarian University of Fine Arts
a. Studio Borzak

## I

040.28:Iboardcast
d. El Miro

112:Id doma
d. Saša Stucin

066.70:Illuminartis
a. Thomas Hirter

203:Interclick
a. CA Square

092.116:Intrum Justitia
a. Dolhem Design

027.07:IPMARK
a. Morillas

037.19:Iskon Broadband Telecom
a. Bunch

188:ITV Studios
a. Mammal

240-241:IVA
a. Make®
cd. Kristoffer Gudbrand
d. Hans Chan, Daniel Flösser

## J

033.15:Jack in the Box
a. Duffy & Partners

147:Jam Factory
a. Canvas Group

109.135:JEAN BOURGET
a. BAYADERES
cd. Françoise Brietzke, Charlotte Vallee

176.78:Jewish Foundation for Education of Women
a. C&G Partners

026:JWI Louvres
a. Canvas Group

## K

161.55:Kallergis Interiors
d. Kanella Arapoglou

222.151:Kaplan Thaler Group
a. C&G Partners

061:Kreditbanken
d. Ekaterina Tiouleikina

138:Kura Restaurant
a. Anti/Anti

## L

186.95:Labyrinth Theatre
a. C&G Partners

187.98:La Feliz
a. Negro™

107.132:Launch Collective
a. RoAndCo
cd. Roanne Adams
d. Tadeu Magalhães, Cynthia Ratsabouth

094-095:Lawson-Fenning
a. TomTor Studio

050.47:Le Jardin Moderne
d. Vivien Le Jeune Durhin

058.60:Le Musée Olympique
a. GVA Studio

082:Libreria Formatos Bookstore
a. Xose Teiga Studio

201.116:Library of Congress
a. Chermayeff & Geismar

151.31:Life Uncommon Photography
a. Design Ranch

047.42:Linz
a. máSustancia
d. Lucas D'Amore

032:Little Chef
a. venturethree
cd. Stuart Watson
d. Mark Williams

209.130:LM Wind Powe
a. Make®
cd. Kristoffer Gudbrand, Thomas Hørup
d. Michael Nilsson

140.24:Loteria De Catalunya
a. Morillas

224.158:LSI
a. Liquid Agency
cd. Boyd Tveit

## M

117.145:Made by Humans
a. Sorachief Design Ltd.

089.107:Mannheimer Swartling
a. Dolhem Design

117.147:Maria Pinto
a. TNOP™ DESIGN

182:Mark Warner
a. SomeOne

144-146:Marmalade Toast
a. &Larry
cd. Larry Peh
d. Lee Weicong

169.68:Marta Fernandez
a. Negro™

033.13:MARTINS
a. MANIFIESTO FUTURA

172-173:Massimo
a. NNSS
cd. Tomás Fliess
d. Emiliano Aranguren, Eliana Testa

131:Matias Nadal. Composer
a. Rocío Martinavarro

077:Melazic
a. Blackswan

216-217:Melbourne Convention Exhibition Centre
a. R-Co

086-087:Memoma
a. Memoma

106:Mercato Antiques
a. Design Ranch

152.35:Meredith
a. Lippincott
cd. Connie Birdsall
d. Jenifer Lehker, Sandra Hill

057.56:Metallica
a. Turner Duckworth
cd. David Turner, Bruce Duckworth
ad. Sarah Moffat
d. Jamie McCathie

192.105 :MIB
a. Stas Sipovich

210.132:Microspray
a. NNSS
cd. Tomás Fliess
d. Tomás Fliess, Nicolás Gloazzo

160:Mindshare
a. Moving Brands

222.152:Minstrel
a. Floor Wesseling

125.152:Mittongtare Studio
a. TomTor Studio

174-175:MK Bergen
a. Grandpeople

202.121:MMCD
a. F1RSTDESIGN

090.109:Mobil Oil Corporation
a. Chermayeff & Geismar

139.21:Moku
a. DTM_INC

101:Monarch Airlines
a. Interbrand
cd. Gion-Men Kruegel-Hanna(Executive), David Jenkinson

076.89:Monterossa
a. RAINERI DESIGN

071.82:Montreux Cafe
a. BÜRO UFHO
ad. JUN
d. Yana

238.08:Moreton Bay & Islands
a. Interbrand

178:MTV Push
a. Studio Hansa
cd. Nick scott
ad. Chris Angelkov
p. Felix Weidemann
a. MTV World Design Studio
cd. Roberto Bagatti (MTV)
ad. Carlos Carrasco, Anna Caregnato
Previous logo credit: Eloisa Iturbe Studio.

080-081:Murmure
a. Murmure

157.46:MyDesign
d. Kanella Arapoglou

205:My Eskimo Friend
a. TomTor Studio

N

201.118:National Library of Ireland
a. Creative Inc.

111:National Maritime Museum
a. SomeOne

200.114:NBC Universal
a. Wolff Olins
cd. Todd Simmons
d. Mike Abbink, Paul van der Laan

208.127:New French Bakery
a. Duffy & Partners

170.71:New Look
a. SomeOne

124:New Readymade Projects
d. Alex Lin

224.157:New York State Restaurant Association
a. C&G Partners

089.106:NightHawk
a. OVO

260:Nike 5
a. Floor Wesseling

038.23:Niko
a. Duval Guillaume Corporate
d. Henk Willems

191:Noeeko
a. Noeeko

O

232-235:OCAD University
a. Bruce Mau Design

036:OIC
a. Blackswan

024.03:ÒMNIUM llengua Cultura País.
a. Morillas

058.59:Olympic Air
a. Company

239:Ookla
a. TNOP™ DESIGN

161.57:Optima
a. Duval Guillaume Corporate
d. Henk Willems

084.101:OSBORNE
a. Morillas

P

040.29:Palm
a. Turner Duckworth
cd. David Turner, Bruce Duckworth
d. David Turner, Jonathan Warner

108:Parad
a. Proekt Communication Agency
cd. Roman Krikheli
d. Andrey Koodenko, Dmitry Rybalkin
c. Ivan Popov

153:Patria
a. Brandient
d. Cristian 'Kit' Paul, Alin Tamasan, Iancu Barbarasa

122-123:Penduka Namibia
a. Buro Reng

043.34:Peter Bailey
a. Bunch 190 Pfingstaffel Thomas Hirter

109.134:Pitcher & Piano
a. Studio Output

148:Pizzeria Delfina
d. Gaston Yagmourian, Andy Baron, Ken Frederick

059.61:Prodigius Cinema
d. David Torrents

212:Promenade
a. Designers Journey

084.102:PronoKal
a. Morillas

041.30:Probst
d. Thomas Hirter

225:Pula is More
a. Parabureau

Q

158.48:Qval
d. Gaston Yagmourian

R

043.35:RBA
a. Morillas

169.67:Rebecca Turbow
a. RoAndCo
cd. Roanne Adams
d. Tadeu Magalhães, Cynthia Ratsabouth

157.45:Reddingsbrigade
a. Calango

158.47:Regional Arts Victoria
a. Studio Brave

139.20:Restaurante Natália
d. Carlos Ribeiro

056.55:Rewind
a. Saša Stucin

024.04:Rosendahl
a. Make®
cd. Kristoffer Gudbrand
d. Daniel Flösser, Michael Nilsson

110.137:RPW Law
d. Garrett Patz

S

067.73:S4C
a. Proud Creative

179.83:Sabotage
a. Floor Wesseling

089.108:Samuels Yoelin Kantor LLP
a. Jeff Fisher LogoMotives
d. Jeff Fisher

222.153:San Bernardino
a. Blumagenta

185:Sankeys Club
a. Yolo Ltd.
d. Martin Fewell

166:San Pellegrino Terme
a. Caselli Associates

069.75:Sanico
a. Lavernia & Cienfuegos Design

097.122:Sanipur
a. RAINERI DESIGN

113.142:Sara Merz Photography
a. We Love Moules Frites

186.96:Saturday Sessions
a. Studio Output

039.26:Sati
a. Raf Vancampenhoudt

156.44:Savana
a. Brandient
d. Cristian 'Kit' Paul, Alin Tamasan

201.117:SETI Institute
a. Turner Duckworth
cd. David Turner, Bruce Duckworth
d. David Turner, Sara Geroulis, Jonathan Warner

134.12:SHOT
a. MANIFIESTO FUTURA

126.01:Shine
a. Studio Output

221.150:Shitang Management
a. Resonance
d. Dai Fan, Wang Xiaoxue

043.36:SKOLV
a. Thomas Hirter

046:Sky
a. venturethree
cd. Paul Townsin, Graham Jones

060.65:Smartree
a. Brandient
d. Cristian 'Kit' Paul

215.140:Spackman Mossop and Michaels
d. Erik Kiesewetter, Maria Hinds

030-031:Spudbar
a. Truly Deeply
cd. David Ansett
ad. Cassandra Gill
d. Lachlan McDougall, Cassandra Gill
t. Lachlan McDougall, Cassandra Gill
i. Veronica Fever
c. Dave Ansett, Peter Singline
Finish Artist: Rachel O'Brien

090.111:St George International
a. Mammal

045:Star Plus
a. venturethree
cd. Stuart Jane
d. Jason Lowings

164:STEM Ambassadors
a. Purpose

027.09:SuperD
a. MetaDesign

027.08:SVEDKA
a. Established

165.61:Swiss Institute of Bioinformatics
a. blue-infinity
cd. Edwin Hassink
d. Edwin Hassink

133:Swisscom
a. Moving Brands

156.42:Syfy
a. Proud Creative

156.46:Sygma Bank
a. BNA

# T

132.09:Tasmania
a. R-Co

152.34:Tassimo
a. Turner Duckworth
cd. David Turner, Bruce Duckworth
ad. Mark Waters
d. Mark Waters, Miles Marshall, John Hughes, David Germain

071.81:Teethwhite
a. El Studio

187.97:Tenso
a. Negro

170.72:Tessa
a. másSustancia
d. Lucas D'Amore

134.14:The Consortium for Street Children
a. Purpose

062-064:The Girl Scouts of the USA
a. The Original Champions of Design
d. Bobby C. Martin Jr, Jennifer Kinon
i. Jasper Goodall, Joe Finocchiaro

107.131:The Cradle
a. Truly Deeply
cd. David Ansett
ad. David Ansett, Cassandra Gill
d. Cassandra Gill
t. Cassandra Gill
i. Cassandra Gill
c. Dave Ansett, Peter Singline
Finish Artist: Rachel O'Brien

168:The Great Blandini
a. Interbrand

070.79:The Irish Greyhound Board
a. Creative Inc.

151.32:The Island of the Bahamas
a. Duffy & Partners

034-035:The Marmalade Pantry
a. &Larry
cd. Larry Peh
d. Lee Weicong

028-029:The PURE Water Co.
a. Neue Design Studio
p. Studio Dreyer Hensley, Thomas Brun
Product Design: Scandinavian Design Group

261:The Tracks
d. Andre Weier

083.99:The Viral Company
a. Become

160.53:The Women's Tennis Association
a. Chermayeff & Geismar

219.145:The Y
a. Siegel+Gale

107.130:Thymes
a. Duffy & Partners

092.115:Time Warner Cable
a. The Brand Union
cd. Wally Krantz Jr
ad. Sam Becker

117.146:Tine Kozjak
d. Saša Stucin

064-066:TMF Awards
d. John Beckers

072:85:Topagunea
a. di-da komunikakzioa

047.44:TPG
a. GVA Studio

162-163:Tramelan
a. onlab

181:Tunerfish
a. Liquid Agency

213.138:Twist & Tango
d. Nicklas Hultman

# U

179.81:U-Rock
a. Hula + Hula
d. Aldo Lugo

079.93:UK Skills
a. Purpose

038.22:UniGeo
a. Haltenbanken

# V

125.153:Vassdal & Eriksen
a. Haltenbanken

120-121:VdpArchitecten
a. Buro Reng

183.89:Vinger
a. Floor Wesseling

050.49:VideoGamer.com
a. Just Creative Design

184.93:Vinylhund
a. Henrik Gytz

093.118:Voices of Youth
a. Hyperakt
cd. Deroy Peraza, Julia Vakser Zeltser
d. Deroy Peraza, Julia Vakser Zeltser, Jason Lynch

254-255:VPRO
a. Thonik

167.64:Vrionis Music House
a. ChrisTrivizas

100:VYP
a. NNSS
cd. Tomás Fliess
d. Andrés Humenczuk

# W

040.27:Wanjia Media Group
a. MetaDesign

126.02:Water for People
a. Duffy & Partners

226-227:Waterstone's
a. venturethree
cd. Stuart Jane
d. Grant Dickson, Jason Lowings, Mark Williams

110.138:Where They At
a. Erik Kiesewetter

139.19:Wolfgang Puck
a. Duffy & Partners

126.03:Worldreader
a. Caselli Associates

# X

221.148:Xingu Commercial 06 Exhibition
a. Resonance
d. Dai Fan, Wang Xiaoxue

# Y

060.63:Yarra Trams
a. R-Co

242-243:Your Singapore.com
a. BBH Asia Pacific.

# Z

044.39:ZARAGOZA Ayuntamiento
a. Morillas

183. 90:Zeeburgia
a. Floor Wesseling

209.129:Zefiro
a. Blumagenta

220:Zhengwei Group
a. Resonance
d. Dai Fan, Wang Xiaoxue

050.48:ZUMBI
a. Calango

# :ACKNOWLEDGEMENTS

We would like to thank all the designers for their kind permission to publish their works, as well as all the photographers who have generously granted us the rights to use their images. We are also very grateful to many other people whose names do not appear on the credits but who made specific contributions and provided support. Without them, we would not be able to share these beautiful redesigned logos with readers around the world.